MID-AMERICA WALKING ATLAS

MID-AMERICA WALKING ATLAS

Gary Yanker
and Carol Tarlow

McGRAW-HILL PUBLISHING COMPANY

New York   St. Louis   San Francisco   Bogotá
Hamburg   Madrid   Mexico   Milan   Montreal
Paris   São Paulo   Tokyo   Toronto

WALKING WORLD STAFF

Editors: Gary Yanker and Carol Tarlow
Managing Editor: Katherine Burton
Map Illustrator: Barbara Frake
Map Editors: Elina Lowensohn and Susan Henricks
Researchers: Dalia Kandiyoti, Linda Filchev, and Linda Ravin
Business Manager: Kelly C. Kane

Walking Atlas® is a trademark of Walking World.

1 2 3 4 5 6 7 8 9 FGR FGR 8 9 2 1 0 9

ISBN 0-07-072233-1

LIBRARY OF CONGRESS CATALOGING-IN-PUBLICATION DATA

Yanker, Gary.
   Mid-America walking atlas / Gary Yanker and Carol Tarlow.
    p. cm.
   ISBN 0-07-072233-1
   1. Hiking—Middle West—Guide-books.   2. Walking—Middle West—Guide-books.   3. Middle West—Description and travel—Guide-books.
I. Tarlow, Carol.   II. Title.
GV199.42.M53Y36 1989
917.8—dc19   88-28209
                                              CIP

Book design by Sheree Goodman.

Contents

Introduction

DRIVE/WALK AMERICA

Wanderlust, a phenomenon which has probably been part of the American psyche since the Pilgrims landed at Plymouth Rock, is at an all-time high in the United States. Americans, who were a little hesitant to jump into their cars for long drives during the oil crisis of the 1970s, are rediscovering the joys of driving. At the same time, perhaps with an eye on better fitness and good health, they have pushed walking into *first place* as their favorite exercise and recreational activity, according to the Bureau of the Census.

Combining walking and driving, while fairly new to the United States, has been common practice in Europe and countries such as New Zealand for many years. As you drive along certain highways in Europe, for example, you'll find rest stops where you can park your car and take a walk along a marked trail. At the Trailhead, a sign provides a map and indicates the distance of the walk, the approximate walking time, and the level of difficulty. In Austria and New Zealand, you can walk from city to city on specially created interconnecting walking routes.

Driving and walking are a good combination. Driving expands your walking horizons. You can "fast-forward" over areas you don't want to walk and spend more time enjoying those you do. Walking gives you an "intimate" view and a sense of place not attainable from a car that is whooshing along a highway. Getting out of your car, planting your feet solidly on the ground, taking a deep breath, and absorbing the sights and sounds around you can be an exhilarating experience and is, according to many, the best part of a travel day.

We hope to propel the walking movement in America toward a complete "foot network" across the United States with our *Walking Atlas of America* series. We started the process with *America's Greatest Walks* (Addison-Wesley, 1986) by placing signs at the beginning of some of the 100 walking routes described in that book.

Now we present 100 new walks in each region of the country: *Mid-America Walking Atlas*, *New England Walking Atlas*, and *California Walking Atlas*. Like the walk-route signs in Europe, these books provide a tableau of important information. Each description is accompanied by explicit driving directions from major roadways and cities, the approximate walking time, the mileage of the walk, the difficulty of the walk, and the best season to take it. One day we hope all the trails will be marked with our signs as part of a walking network, reaching across the country.

If you haven't yet made walking a daily habit on your business and vacation travels, here are our recommendations for fitting in a "walk a day":

- *Build time for a walk into your travel schedule by starting an hour earlier.* You'll be surprised how this extra margin will help you take advantage of an unplanned walking opportunity.

- *Be "walk-ready" at all times.* Wear walking shoes, socks, and comfortable clothing. Some people prefer to carry a backpack instead of a briefcase or pocketbook so they can take a walking break at a moment's notice. At any rate, travel "light."

- *Make a daily walk plan (even if it's only mental).* Think about each day, and decide when you *might* be able to take time out for a walk. Will it be in the morning before breakfast near your hotel? Can you walk to an appointment? Is there time at lunch? Before dinner? Maybe a "walking" meeting with a business associate? If you target the day's possible walking opportunities, you are more likely to actually find time to take your walk.

- *Be spontaneous.* Travelers—even though in the abstract they are seeking a pleasant escape or an exciting discovery—can get into a rut. The destination looms larger than the journey itself. Allow yourself the luxury of leaving your route, parking your car, and exploring a new area on foot.

MID-AMERICA'S 100 BEST WALKS

While there are thousands of marked and unmarked walks to choose from, we have tried to present the best walks (or at least those which are the best-loved) by asking walkers across Mid-America to nominate their favorites, using a nomination form like the one in the back of this book. In this way we have created a personal, "democratic" walking atlas, a book that is, in the words of Mid-America's most famous citizen, "of the people, by the people and for the people."

And what a people! We were astounded by the response we received to our requests for nominations and by the enthusiasm so many Americans have for their particular corner of the world. Whether you take one of these walks, several of them, all of them, or none at all, we are certain you will enjoy reading about them. Jan Moritz and Dick Zlab, for example, invite you to take their Winsome Woods Walk in eastern Nebraska, where "nature encompasses and holds every living thing in a time warp, if only for a few precious moments." Robert Buntz, Jr., describes a wonderful walk he and his wife Mary took in the Sawtooth Mountains of Minnesota, above Lake Superior. One of the most enthusiastically endorsed walks is the Rock Island Trail in central Illinois, which received three separate nominations as best walk. As its name suggests, the trail follows an abandoned railroad right-of-way through a scenic prairie setting which leads to the picturesque Spoon River Valley. And there's the Puddle-Jumper Trail in northwest Iowa, which also follows an old railroad bed. Doris Vogel, who told us about it, says, "There's nothing better than a vigorous walk on the Puddle-Jumper!"

There are city walks, too. A great one in Indianapolis, and perhaps one you didn't know about in Chicago. And, even if you can't get to New Orleans, you'll love J. Michael Kenny's affectionate "new look at the Old Quarter" and walk along the Bayou St. John Waterway. There's a city walk in every state from Bismarck, North Dakota, to Shreveport, Louisiana; from Wichita, Kansas, to Little Rock, Arkansas. Don't forget to pack us along the next time you take a trip!

Last, but certainly not least, you'll find that many of these walks are "easy-to-take" courses in subjects such as history, geography, geology, sociology, ecology, and environmental studies. Mid-America is rich in Indian heritage, for example, and you'll learn some things about Indian history you may not have known on such walks as the Trail of the Spirits in northeast South Dakota, the Fort Omaha walk in Nebraska, the Lake Shetek walk in southwest Minnesota, or the walk through a "living museum,"—the Cherokee village, Tsa-La-Gi,—in Oklahoma. In the Cimarron National Grasslands in southwestern Kansas, you'll retrace the footsteps of the pioneers who rode the Santa Fe Trail, and on the Saddle Rock Trail on the western edge of Nebraska's panhandle, you'll walk in the ruts of the wagons along the Oregon Trail. On the Jones Creek Trail in western North Dakota, you'll be amazed, as the pioneers were, at the sight of the incongruous and forbidding, moonlike landscape of the Badlands. And, perhaps, you may even be inspired to create your own "personal heritage" walk as Margaret Webster did in east central Minnesota, where she traced her roots and created a walk in the footsteps of her own ancestors.

Geology comes to life on such walks as the Parnell Tower Loop off the Ice Age Trail in southeastern Wisconsin, where you can view glacial topography and witness firsthand the incredible power of the Ice Age glaciers. Several of the walks pass through wildlife sanctuaries, such as the Marsh Trail in the Sabine Wildlife Refuge near Sulphur, Louisiana, and the walk through the Sand Lake Wildlife Refuge in northeastern South Dakota. In these special areas, you can learn more about the challenges to all of us in our attempts to preserve vanishing species. And in the numerous garden walks, like the one in the Dawes Arboretum near Columbus, Ohio, there is an abundance of information about plant and animal life and an opportunity to observe the delicate relationship that exists between people and their environment.

There are one or two walks in this book, like the 200-mile North Country Trail in Michigan's Upper Peninsula, that are only for the experienced hiker. Donald Weiss sent us a description of his fourteen-day trek on this trail, and he prefaced it with a list of seven essentials: good health, top mental and physical condition, understanding family, ironclad desire to succeed, advance planning, good equipment, and good luck!

Most of the walks presented here, however, are short and easy and can be enjoyed by young and old alike. Some people, like Janet Delkus of Collinsville, Illinois, use their walk to get an aerobic workout. Nancy Goodman and Patty Peery of Lancaster, Ohio, combine exercise and history on their walks through Forest Rose Cemetery.

And if you are ever in Beloit, Wisconsin, you'll want to join Roger Schwebke on his walk through the Beloit Mall. According to Roger it is, quite simply: "The best place in town to walk." You'll get a chance to visit with the "regulars" like Roger, who often meet at various "walkers' gathering places" for a cup of coffee and some good talk.

In sum, this very personal walking atlas brings us closer to our country and to the people who live in it. Our thanks to all of you who nominated walks and to all of you who will take them.

If you have a favorite walk that you would like to share, please complete the form at the end of the book and send it to us. We'd also appreciate any suggestions or updated information you might have on the walks in this book.

The maps are meant to give you a general orientation to each new area. We suggest you obtain more detailed information locally when you arrive, to ensure that you make the most of your visit. There are many self-guided tour brochures and trail guides which will enhance your walks.

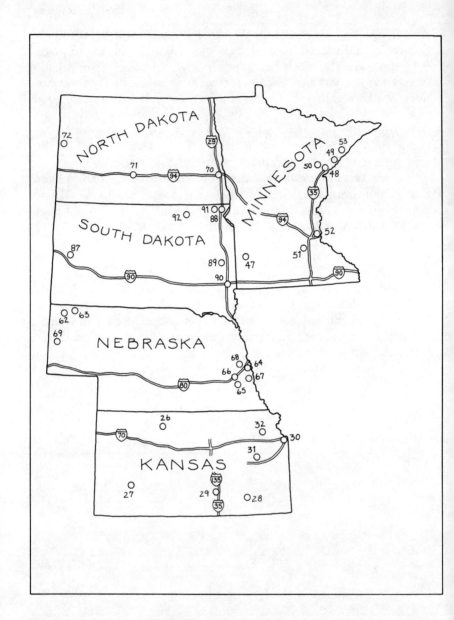

Northern Mid-America

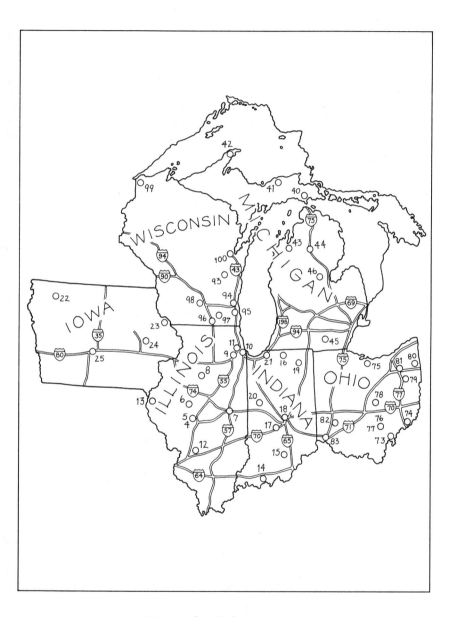

Central Mid-America

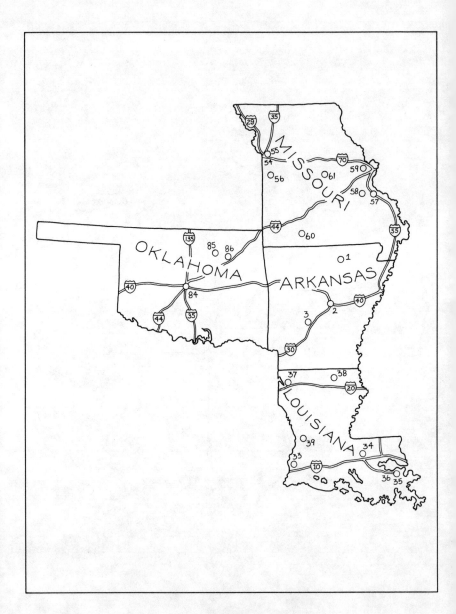

Southern Mid-America

NORTHERN ARKANSAS

Indian Rockhouse Trail (1)

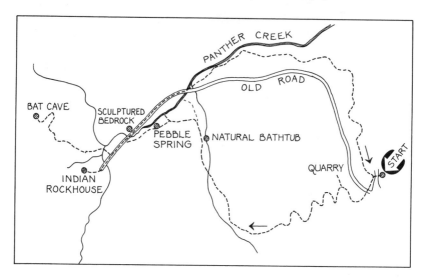

Directions: The trail is located at Buffalo Point in Buffalo National River, a two- to three-hour drive from Little Rock and Fayetteville, Arkansas, or Springfield, Missouri. Buffalo Point is located off Arkansas Highway 14, 17 miles south of Yellville.

Best Season: Year-round. Nominator Rich McCamant, chief interpreter at Buffalo National River, prefers winter, because with no leaves on the trees there are more open vistas. He also likes spring for all the wildflowers.

Length: 3 miles to the "rockhouse" and back.

Degree of Difficulty: Moderate. Pace yourself—the return trip is uphill.

Highlights: Rock caves that housed Indians more than 8,000 years ago, a side trip to Bat Cave, and an abandoned zinc mine are highlights of this walk.

There are 95,000 acres within Buffalo National River, nestled in the Arkansas Ozarks, and much of it is almost exactly as it was when only the Indians walked here. Geographically and ecologically isolated, the Buffalo River Valley is a "living biological museum with silent bluffs for walls."

Two trails go off at slight angles at the Trailhead. Take the right, or lower, one, which passes through a hardwood forest of oaks, elms, and hickories, as well as numerous deciduous hardwoods and then a small cedar glade. Soon you'll come to a waterfall and then an abandoned zinc mine. Zinc was discovered in the area around 1880, and when its value soared during World War I, many people began prospecting their own lands. Most of the mines, like the one you see here, were empty of minable zinc and were soon abandoned. Nominator Rich McCamant says, "If you look closely you'll see evidence of the miners' presence, including a few foundations of homesites and plants such as daffodils which miners planted around their homes." Today deer mice, woodrats, and cave salamanders use the abandoned mines for their homes.

Now the trail joins Panther Creek, which leads to the Indian Rockhouse. The creek, dry most of the year, becomes a raging torrent after heavy rain. Once past a small cave, you'll see a trail on your right. This leads to Bat Cave, but it's not an easy walk. The trail has suffered badly from erosion and is rough and steep. Don't attempt it if you've had any trouble at all hiking up to this point. The Bat Cave Trail crosses Panther Creek and climbs to the top of a ridge where flowering pink azaleas bloom in the spring and from which there is a scenic view in winter. You can enter the Bat Cave to about 100 feet, but at that point, passage has been blocked by a huge landslide.

Back on the Indian Rockhouse Trail, you'll come now to the "rockhouse" itself. According to Rich, it is more accurately described as a bluff shelter of limestone and sandstone "big enough to hold a football field." Archaeologists excavating the area have found evidence that cave-dwelling Indians lived here between 8,000 and 10,000 years ago.

The return trip begins here. Follow the old roadbed back over the hill to the return trail which veers to the right.

CENTRAL ARKANSAS

Little Rock: The Quapaw Quarter (2)

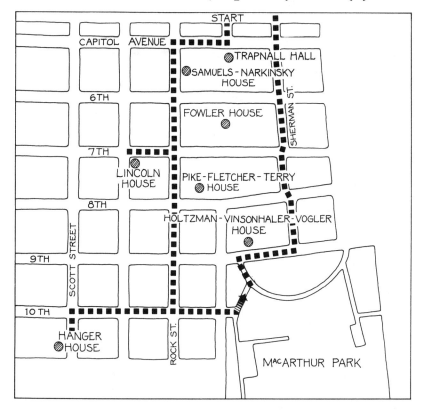

Directions: Located in downtown Little Rock, this walk begins at Trapnall Hall, 423 E. Capitol Avenue.

Best Season: Spring and fall.

Length: Allow half a day for this walk through historic Little Rock.

Degree of Difficulty: Easy.

Highlights: The beautiful stately old homes of Little Rock's past come to life on this elegant tour.

The Quapaw Quarter is named for the Quapaw Indians who once lived in central Arkansas. It owes its existence to farsighted individuals who understood the historical and architectural significance of Little Rock's old buildings and fought to preserve them when the MacArthur Park area of the Quapaw Quarter became part of a huge urban renewal project in the 1960s.

The neighborhood of MacArthur Park began developing in the late 1830s around the same time that a United States arsenal was established in Little Rock. Magnificent homes were built along the streets near the arsenal, and they are the focus of this walking tour, which begins at Trapnall Hall on Capitol Avenue. Built in 1843 by attorney Frederic Trapnall, the house is a wonderful example of the antebellum style. Owned by the State of Arkansas, the house serves today as the Governor's Receiving Hall.

The next home on the walk is the Samuels-Narkinsky House off Capitol Avenue on Rock Street. Built by retail merchant John Samuels, it reflects the Italianate style as does the Kempner House next door. As you walk down Rock Street, you will pass several other impressive houses, but perhaps none quite the equal of the Lincoln House, which you can see from the corner of Rock and Seventh streets. It was built in 1878 and is one of the most important Italianate-style homes in the city. Walk down Seventh to have a closer look.

One of the best-known homes in the district is the Pike-Fletcher-Terry House on the southeast corner of Seventh and Rock. Built in 1840, the house is now a Decorative Arts Museum open daily to the public.

Nominator Hallie Simmins says that all the homes on this walk are fascinating but the most photographed one is the incredibly elegant Hanger House at 1010 Scott Street. The intricate Queen Anne style is the result of an 1889 remodeling job accomplished by Frances and Frederick Hanger.

From Hanger House, walk down Scott to Tenth Street and turn right. Follow Tenth Street into MacArthur Park (named for General Douglas MacArthur, who was born here) where you'll find the Arkansas Arts Center and the Arkansas Museum of Science and History. Both are open daily to the public.

Exit the park on Ninth Street and continue up Sherman Street to find the Holtzman-Vinsonhaler-Vogler House (512 E. Ninth Street), with its magnificent stained-glass window, and the Fowler House (503 E. Sixth Street), another antebellum home built ca. 1840.

CENTRAL ARKANSAS

Hot Springs: Sunset Trail (3)

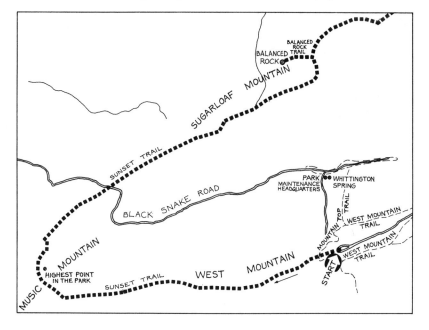

Directions: The Trailhead is located at the West Mountain Summit Overlook in Hot Springs National Park. From Little Rock, take I-30 south to Route 70 east. Drive to Route 7, which leads into the park, and follow signs to the West Mountain Summit Overlook.

Best Season: Year-round.

Length: 8.5 miles one way, though it is possible to hike just parts of the trail.

Degree of Difficulty: Easy to moderate. The terrain slopes gently, but the trail is primitive.

Highlights: Music Mountain, the highest point in the park, and Balanced Rock, where there are magnificent views of the valley.

The Zig Zag Mountains in Hot Springs National Park are erosion-resistant remnants of sandstone and novaculite, a very hard, flint-type stone that has been mined in the area for centuries. Indians used it for arrow- and spearheads and for tools; today novaculite is still mined because it is valued by artisans for whetstones used to sharpen precision tools.

Sunset Trail leads from the West Mountain Summit Overlook to Music Mountain, the highest point in the park and the center of the huge horseshoe-shaped ridge that ends at the Sugarloaf and West mountains. Nominator Gail Sears says there are various overlooks along the trail with views of the city of Hot Springs, Lakes Catherine and Hamilton, and, in the distance, the Trap Mountains.

From Music Mountain, the trail crosses Black Snake Road and leads to the trail marker for Balanced Rock Trail. This quarter-mile trail was also nominated by Earl Adams, who calls it the "most scenic trail in the park." If you want a much shorter walk, you can get to the Balanced Rock Trail from Hot Springs by picking up the Sunset Trail in town instead of walking all the way from the Summit Overlook. After walking on the Sunset Trail for 4/10 of a mile, you'll be at the trail marker for Balanced Rock.

The rock itself, resting on a natural pedestal, is 10 feet high and 5 feet wide and is made of pure white novaculite. From the edge of the gorge you'll have a spectacular view of the valley. "You really get up in the world on this trail," Earl comments. It's a very popular walk. Every October, for example, there's a Volksmarch to the rock. Everyone who completes the walk receives a pin or memento of some sort at the end.

According to both Earl and Gail, fall is a particularly good time to take this walk. In addition to the beautiful fall-blooming flowers and the strawberries, there are the deep colors, the reds and yellows, from the leaves of red oaks and hickories. There is also an Ozark Chinkapin along the trail, Earl says, which is an endangered tree.

After visiting Balanced Rock, return to the Sunset Trail and follow it to the fire gate at Cedar Glades Road. At this point you have hiked 5.65 miles, if you began at the Summit Overlook. You can continue on for about another 3 miles to the northernmost boundary of the park. If you don't want to retrace your steps all the way back to the Trailhead, you can arrange to have someone meet you at Cedar Glades Road, or you can take the shorter route back to town.

CENTRAL ILLINOIS

Lincoln Memorial Garden
Woodland Walk (4)

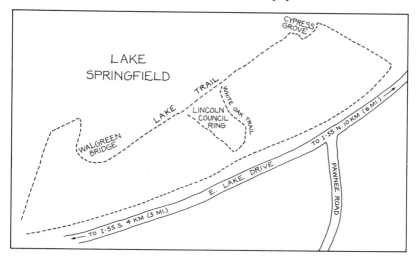

Directions: Take I-55 from Springfield to exit 88, and follow signs to the garden.

Best Season: Year-round, but fall and spring are the most colorful. "There's spectacular color in the fall," says nominator Jim Matheis, "and a profusion of wildflowers and flowering trees in spring."

Length: 1 to 5 miles, depending on how much you want to walk.

Degree of Difficulty: Easy to moderate; there are a few small hills.

Highlights: Sunsets over the lake, ducks in the streams, hawks and owls, and many resting places where you can stop and absorb beautiful vistas of the lake and woods.

"My favorite time to walk in the garden," says Jim Matheis, who told us about this place, "is early in the morning or just before sunset."

Jim likes the early morning because he often sees and hears things that can be missed once the path has had more people on it. "You may surprise the mallards," he says, "as they float silently on one of the small streams which flow throughout the garden, or a great horned owl or red-tailed hawk might glide from a tall oak as you pass close by. If you're lucky you might see a family of deer come down to water or a red fox on his way home after a night of hunting."

Sunset is special because twilight creates a world of enchanting colors and shadows. If you listen carefully, you will hear a host of sounds that occur only at this time as the nocturnal animals begin their rounds.

Every season brings its own specialty to the garden. In spring it's the blossoms—flowering dogwood, redbuds, crabapples, and splashes of wildflowers over the hills and along the paths. In summer, the meadow flowers dominate in vivid purples, yellows, and pinks. Fall means drama, deep golds and oranges as the leaves change, and in winter a soft white blanket sparkles under the sun. The sounds change, too, but there is always something—the songs of birds, the rustle of a chipmunk, the gentle lapping of the lake on the shore.

Jim sent us a poem about the garden, written by a local author. We'd like to share it with you:

"ON THE LINCOLN MEMORIAL GARDEN"

Come...Walk...Sit...Rest...Ponder;
Wander through the Garden,
Let the Garden be absorbed into your being.
Feel the refreshing breeze in your face.
Hear the music of the whirling wind,
The rustling of the leaves.
Listen, the call of the wild bird
Above the roll of the wind.

Go walk along the lake shore,
See the sun glisten on the rippling waves;
Hear the splashing waters against the shore.

Wander through the Garden,
Let the Spirit move you.

Sit on rough hewn benches
Carved with Lincoln's phrases.

Seek the wisdom and balance of his words.
You may become more moderate,
>*patient,*
>>*charitable,*
>>>*strong,*
>>>>*and resolute.*
You may even develop your sense of humor.

Come, let the Spirit move you
In the beauty and wonder
Of the Lincoln Memorial Garden!

by Kenneth Sibley

CENTRAL ILLINOIS

Historic Springfield (5)

Directions: Follow signs to the Visitor's Center in downtown Springfield where you can pick up maps and a brochure for this self-guided walking tour.

Best Season: Spring, summer, fall.

Length: As little as 1½ hours, says nominator Dave Copeland, but you should allow a full day to complete the entire tour.

Degree of Difficulty: Easy.

Highlights: A chance to experience firsthand the town Lincoln loved.

Abraham Lincoln spent twenty-five years in Springfield. He moved there as a young man, he practiced law there, he got married there, and he ran for president while living there. The only home he ever owned is there. It's impossible to walk the streets of Springfield and not be uplifted by the spirit of the man who so loved this place. His fully restored home, which is located in a small park at Seventh and Jackson, has recently been renovated and is open free to the public from 8:30 a.m. to 5:00 p.m. daily.

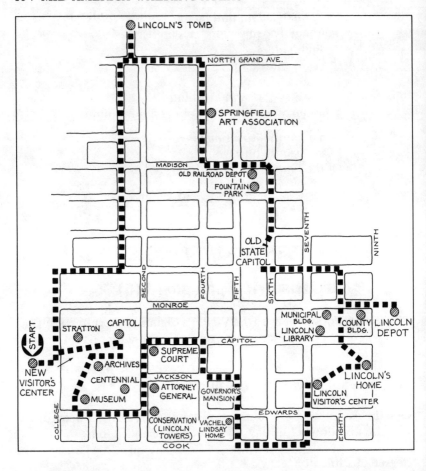

Be sure to visit the Old State Capitol, which contains an original copy of the Gettysburg Address. Here, on weekend evenings from mid-June to mid-August, actors join with the chamber orchestra to recreate the lives of Illinois' most famous residents. Reservations to this memorable production, called "Portrait of a Prairie Capitol," are necessary. Call (217) 785-9363.

Follow Monroe Street and look for the Lincoln Depot, located between Ninth and Tenth Streets. It was from here that Lincoln said good-bye to his beloved Springfield and boarded a train for Washington, D.C., and his inauguration. "No one, not in my situation," he said in his farewell to the people of Springfield, "can appreciate my feeling of sadness at this parting. To this place, and the kindness of these people, I owe everything."

Just north of Springfield, at the end of Monument Boulevard, is the Lincoln Tomb State Historic Site where from June through August, the Illinois Volunteer Infantry, dressed in authentic Civil War uniforms, practice drill movements. Lincoln was buried in the cemetery on May 4, 1865, at the request of his wife. You can see the vault where his body was originally interred, but the President's body is no longer there. His coffin now rests below the surface of the floor, moved there when a plot to steal his body was discovered. Today this site is one of the most visited in America, and one of the most revered.

CENTRAL ILLINOIS

New Salem Volkswalk Trail (6)

Directions: From Springfield, take Route 97 to New Salem.

Best Season: October for the fall colors.

Length: 10 kilometers (6.2 miles), about 2 hours.

Degree of Difficulty: Moderately difficult. The trail is slippery when wet, and there are two narrow, steep hills.

Highlights: A scenic walk through history.

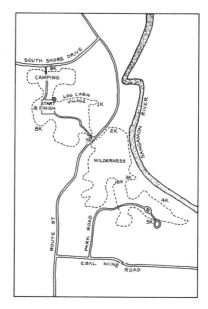

Before or after a visit to Lincoln's Springfield, a trip to New Salem gives the visitor an opportunity to see where Lincoln spent six years of his youth. Here he was a shopkeeper, a postmaster, a surveyor, a member of the Illinois

General Assembly, and a captain in the Black Hawk War. Just north of New Salem in Riverfront Park, there's a monument commemorating Lincoln's return home from that war. And, because of the careful restoration of the New Salem State Historic Site, today's visitor can see the place much as Lincoln did.

The 10-kilometer Volkswalk ("People Walk") Trail, nominated by Roger Mollett, takes the walker through a log cabin village which in every detail is similar to the one in which Lincoln gave up his life as an "aimless piece of driftwood" and began to study law. As you tour the village, you'll hear the blacksmith's hammer and watch the candlemakers at work, just as Lincoln must have seen them. The Onstot Cooper Shop, built in 1835, is original.

The walk, which is free to all participants (embroidered patches and event or distance credits are available for a small fee), begins at the New Salem State Park Information Window, located at the east end of the park office building. Here walkers pick up a "start card" which can be punched at various checkpoints along the way. From the Information Window, simply follow the blue signs bearing the symbol of a hiker.

The trail first winds through the camping area of the park, then enters an area of rather dense woods. After passing an old cemetery and the ruins of a log cabin, it crosses Illinois Route 97 and proceeds into another wooded area. There is a very steep hill to climb and then gently rolling hills. Eventually the trail enters the reconstructed village of New Salem where guides dressed in period costume will explain the history of New Salem and demonstrate the business trades and crafts of the era. From the village, follow the trail back to the park office building and return your start card. Even if you don't complete the entire trail, be sure to hand in your card, so that a ranger will not be sent out to look for you.

Along this path, it is very easy to imagine yourself in the world of the 1800s and to appreciate the fact that this place will never change, thanks to the sixteenth president of the United States, whose memory is here forever preserved. And, as you walk this "Land of Lincoln," it would not be inappropriate to ponder some of the words of this great man. Words that, incredibly—sadly—have as much to say to us today as they did to those who listened to them when Lincoln said them.

I have always thought that all men should be free; but if any should be slaves, it should be first those who desire it for others. Whenever I hear anyone arguing for slavery, I feel a strong impulse to see it tried on him personally.

Address to an Indian Regiment
March 17, 1865

And perhaps most memorable of all, the words that Lincoln said no one would remember:

Fourscore and seven years ago our fathers brought forth on this continent a new nation, conceived in Liberty, and dedicated to the proposition that all men are created equal.

Now we are engaged in a great civil war, testing whether that nation, or any nation so conceived and so dedicated, can long endure. We are met on a great battlefield of that war. We have come to dedicate a portion of that field, as a final resting place for those who here gave their lives that that nation might live....But, in a larger sense, we cannot dedicate—we cannot consecrate—we cannot hallow—this ground. The brave men, living and dead, who struggled here, have consecrated it far above our poor power to add or detract. The world will little note nor long remember what we say here, but it can never forget what they did here....It is rather for us to be here dedicated to the great task remaining before us—that from these honored dead we take increased devotion to that cause for which they gave the last full measure of devotion; that we here highly resolve that these dead shall not have died in vain; that this nation, under God, shall have a new birth of freedom; and that government of the people, by the people, for the people, shall not perish from the earth.

Address at Gettysburg
November 19, 1863

CENTRAL ILLINOIS

Robert Allerton Park (7)

Directions: The park is located 30 miles southwest of Urbana-Champaign. Take I-72 to Monticello.

Best Season: Year-round (the park is open from 10 a.m. until dark every day but Christmas and New Year's Day).

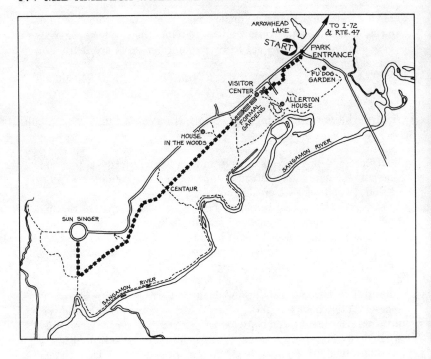

Length: You can spend all day or just an hour or two.

Degree of Difficulty: Moderate.

Highlights: A striking blend of formal gardens with natural woodland habitats.

This diverse and unusual tour of Robert Allerton Park was nominated by David Bowman, who recommends all the many trails that radiate from the Visitor Center and wind throughout the 1,500-acre park. Walkers are encouraged to create their own "tours"; the gardens have entrances and exits at several different locations.

Inspired by the magnificent gardens of England, France, and Germany of the late nineteenth century, the landscaping of the park has a distinctly European flavor. Two stone columns topped with the *Charioteers of Delphi* greet the visitor at the park's main entrance, and not far away is the Fu Dog Garden, where twenty-two blue porcelain Chinese dog statues form a double line in front of a stand of white fir trees. In China, these dogs were thought to keep a home safe—free from fire, flood, earthquake, or other natural disaster.

There are many other statues and sculptures (approaching 100 in total) to surprise and impress you on your walking tour of the park. A mile's walk from the formal gardens, along a scenic forest path, takes you to a most impressive work, *The Death of the Last Centaur*. Erected by Antoine Bourdelle, it symbolizes the death of paganism. Perhaps the most popular work/setting in the park is Carl Mille's *The Sun Singer*, which rises 30 feet from the ground in the middle of a meadow. The statue represents the sun god Apollo; it faces east toward the rising sun and is captured in silhouette as the sun sets.

During your walk through the park, be sure to take a close look at Allerton House, which is located near the Sangamon River. The imposing Georgian mansion, inspired by Ham House in Surrey, England, overlooks a reflecting pool and meadow. Two Italian caryatids (statues of a woman's head and upper torso carved into a stone column) decorate the east side of the house, and two heads of the god Pan are carved into the southwestern walls. The house and ancillary structures serve as a conference center for the University of Illinois, which received the park as a donation from the late Robert Allerton (1873–1964) in 1946. In addition to being a public park, Allerton's gift is used by the university for teaching and research, as a plant and wildlife reserve, and as an example of landscape gardening.

Robert Allerton's father, Samuel, a founder of the Chicago Union Stockyards and the First National Bank of Chicago, acquired the land in the 1800s. When Robert inherited it, he determined to create a "gentleman's country estate." Today this magnificent park is largely the result of his efforts and those of his adopted son, John Gregg Allerton.

CENTRAL ILLINOIS

Rock Island Trail (8)

Directions: The trail begins a few miles north of Peoria in Alta. Take Route 6 north from Peoria to Allen Road (N) to Shamrock Plastics Company at 2615 W. Alta Road. The Trailhead begins just north of the parking lot.

Best Season: Year-round; wildflowers and the blossoms of the chokeberry and wild plum are abundant in spring; wild strawberries and blueberries and a profusion of prairie flowers line the trail in summer; a blaze of fall colors and wild grapes highlight the autumn; the cross-country skiing is wonderful in winter.

Length: 26.5 miles one way. Allow a full day, with a stop for lunch in one of the small towns along the way.

Degree of Difficulty: Easy to moderate. There are some slight hills, but the path will be fully maintained once it is completed in its entirety in the summer of 1989. The grade is not greater than 3 percent at any point.

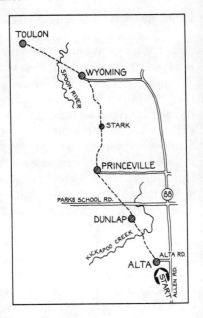

Highlights: A panorama of prairie life both past and present in a scenic setting which encompasses meadows, cornfields, creeks, the Spoon River Valley, a protective canopy of trees, as well as quaint towns.

This 100-foot-wide trail, which links Alta with Toulon, follows an abandoned railroad right-of-way that once belonged to the Rock Island and Pacific Railroad. You can hike the entire trail or take it in segments. The first open segment, 3 miles, runs from Alta to Kickapoo Creek; the second open segment of 6 miles runs from just north of Dunlap to Princeville; the third open segment of 4 to 5 miles links Wyoming and Toulon and passes through the beautiful Spoon River Valley. By the summer of 1989 the entire length of the trail will be covered with crushed limestone screenings and the missing bridges will be replaced.

Referred to as the "orphan park," the Rock Island Trail State Park was made possible by the collective efforts of people in the area. When development of the trail was terminated by the state in 1975, local organizations banded together to ensure its completion. Today the trail is a great source of pride to those who made it possible and a reminder to everyone of what can be accomplished by citizens united in community spirit. The trail received three nominations as "best walk." One from George Burrier, who calls it "a day's worth of beautiful scenery and interesting little towns," one from Teri Stella, and one from Paula Hudachko.

From Alta, the trail crosses over Kickapoo Creek. Here it climbs about 30 to 40 feet. Watch for beaver dams in the many creeks, and don't be surprised if a rabbit or two or a covey of quail decide to join you.

From Kickapoo Creek, follow the trail to Dunlap, where you can stop for a snack or for lunch, depending on the time. North of Dunlap the trail continues on to Princeville and then to Stark, a small prairie village with a few scattered homes. You'll find the contrasting scenery all along the trail a very pleasant diversion. From under a canopy of beautiful trees, for example, you will suddenly find yourself in an open meadow or amid miles of corn and soybean fields.

After the village of Stark, the next town is Wyoming, where you'll pass the Chicago, Burlington & Quincy Railway Company's wooden-frame depot which was built in 1871 and placed on the *National Register of Historic Places* on April 30, 1987, as a result of the efforts of the Friends of the Rock Island Trail, Inc. It should be completely restored by the summer of 1989.

In Wyoming you'll find a collection of false-front stores and restaurants. Pick up the trail again just northwest of where Route 91 turns west to Toulon in downtown Wyoming. This last stretch from Wyoming to Toulon is perhaps the most picturesque of all. A steel bridge that was saved through the intervention of William Rutherford of the Forest Park Foundation spans the Spoon River and affords a wonderful view of the Spoon River Valley, immortalized by Edgar Lee Masters in *Spoon River Anthology*. You can almost hear the voices in these poems as you contemplate the river from this quiet spot. "Small villages and vales such as the ones on this trail," says nominator Paula Hudachko, "still possess many of the characteristics that were present more than seventy years ago when Masters wrote about them."

Nominator George Burrier suggests that before leaving the area you also walk the presently open portions of the Pimiteoui Trail, which begins at the southern entrance of Grandview Drive and extends to Forest Park Nature Center. The trail gives the walker fantastic views of the Illinois River and Peoria Lake. *Pimiteoui* means "fat lake" in the language of the Peoria Indians. There are plans to connect this 9.5 mile trail, which follows a portion of the old Peoria and Galena Coach and Stage Road, with the Rock Island Trail State Park.

NORTHEASTERN ILLINOIS

Riverside, a "Village in a Park" (9)

Directions: From downtown Chicago, take I-290 west for 9 miles. Go south on Harlem Avenue for 3 miles to Riverside. Commuter trains to Riverside also run from downtown Chicago.

Best Season: Year-round.

Length: 1 or 2 miles; allow one to three hours.

Degree of Difficulty: Easy.

Highlights: Fascinating architecture in a historic, pastoral setting.

Nominator Jerome Balin enthusiastically recommends a walk through the lovely and historic town of Riverside, which, according to Walter Creese in his book, *The Crowning of American Landscape*, is one of the eight greatest "spaces" in the United States.

Designed by landscape architect Frederick Law Olmsted and his partner, Calvert Vaux, Riverside is a continuing testament to the huge contribution Olmsted made to the American landscape. The creator of Central Park in New York, Golden Gate Park in San Francisco, and myriad other oases of green throughout the country, Olmsted set out to make Riverside, the nation's first planned suburban community, a "village in a park," as different from Chicago as possible. He and Vaux designed tree-lined carriageways along the gently curving Des Plaines River, which winds through Riverside. They set these roadways lower than the surrounding lawns and parks in order to create a visually undisturbed expanse of greenery. As you walk along

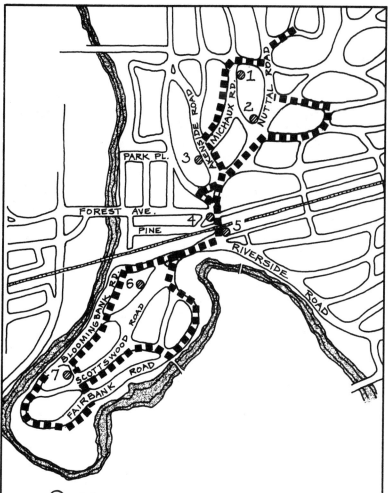

1. 185 MICHAUX RD., Wᴹ· LᵉBARON JENNEY, ARCH.
2. 150 NUTTAL RD., FRANK LLOYD WRIGHT, ARCH.
3. 110 AKENSIDE RD., JENNEY, ARCHITECT
4. RIVERSIDE MUSEUM
5. 1 RIVERSIDE RD., ARCADE BUILDING
6. 124 SCOTTSDALE, JENNEY, ARCHITECT
7. 300 SCOTTSWOOD, AVERY COONLEY RESI-
       DENCE, FRANK LLOYD WRIGHT, ARCH.

the river, imagine it 200 years ago when it was a highway for the Indians and later for the fur traders. Stop by the Riverside Museum for an in-depth look at the town's history.

Today the residents of Riverside go about their twentieth-century business amid gas-lit streets and stately homes, designed by America's foremost architects including Frank Lloyd Wright, Louis Sullivan, and William LeBaron Jenney. There is a wide diversity of architectural styles ranging from Swiss Gothic and Queen Anne to Prairie and Contemporary. The Riverside Historical Commission has identified fifty-two significant structures, including the 1871 Arcade Building, which nominator Jerome Balin tells us is a prototype for today's indoor shopping mall, and the 1908 Coonley Estate, which Frank Lloyd Wright declared one of his finest creations.

Riverside is proof of Olmsted's belief that a peaceful, beautiful environment can have a positive effect on one's spirit. It is a place warm with community feelings and annual civic events such as summer concerts in the park and a popular Christmas Walk. Specialty shops abound—a stained-glass studio, fudge shop, antique store, bakery—and you'll want to stop for lunch or dinner at one of the many wonderful ethnic restaurants. Take time, too, to visit the world-renowned Brookfield Zoo, which houses the impressive Seven Seas and Tropic World exhibits.

Riverside is enveloped by a 1,000-acre lush nature preserve, so walkers share this special place with ducks, geese, deer, raccoons, and opossum. Jerome Balin fittingly concludes: "It's a tribute to Frederick Law Olmsted that the historic, architectural, and aesthetic beauty of Riverside is as much in evidence today as it was in 1871."

NORTHEASTERN ILLINOIS

Chicago River Trail (10)

Directions: To pick up the trail on Chicago's north side, take I-94 to Peterson Avenue (U.S. 14). Go east 2 miles to McCormick Boulevard, and park. The river is less than one block south. To enter the trail from the south side, take I-55 to California Avenue and drive north a half mile to 31st Street. Park, and walk east along the river.

Best Season: Year-round.

Length: 30 miles. Make a whole day of it; there's lots to see and many wonderful places to stop and eat.

Degree of Difficulty: Easy.

Highlights: A rich, diverse urban walk along the Chicago River.

"The Chicago River Trail is like a necklace strung with many beads of different colors, sizes, and shapes," says David Jones, who is the spokesperson for the nominators of this walk, members of the River Trail Committee, Friends of the Chicago River. "Some of the beads are old," David says, "others are brand-new. They are strung in random patterns, yet the overall effect is one of richness, diversity, and intimacy."

The walk begins at a waterfall and follows the river in a "shoelace" pattern through the city, in and out of tree-studded parks, past Beaux Arts sewage pumping stations, through charming neighborhoods, boatyards, and skyscrapers, and back and forth through the Loop, crossing many of the city's 53 movable bridges and passing by numerous sites of interest, including the IBM Building, designed by Mies van der Rohe, the Sears Tower (the world's tallest building), the Wrigley Building, old rail yards, and a number of ethnic neighborhoods, including Chinatown and Pilsen (a Mexican neighborhood with a large artists' colony). The restaurants in these and other ethnic Chicago neighborhoods are not to be missed!

One of the best things about this walk, according to David Jones, is its appeal to the senses: "The smells of the Richheimer Coffee Company, the Blommer Chocolate Factory, the Holsum Bakery and Michaelsky's Bakery, the neighborhood sounds of children and dogs at play, the clickety sounds of a train, the bittersweet sounds of Renato Scotto's aria at the end of Act I of *Tosca* drifting from the open doors of the Opera House."

Although the trail attracts walkers year-round, enjoyment is highlighted during special seasonal celebrations. On St. Patrick's Day, for example, the river turns green as the Irish (and all those who join them for the festivities) throw green dye into the waters (it's back to normal by the next day). On Yom Kippur, Orthodox Jews on the north side gather along the banks of the river to pray that the waters will carry away the sins and mistakes of the previous year. On the second Sunday of October, the Iron Oars Marathon runs from the North Shore Channel, down the river to the lakefront. There are special events and celebrations in practically every month!

"The river is a connector," explains David. "It connects diverse neighborhoods one to another, it connects the north side of the city to the south side. It connects the Mississippi River Drainage Basin to the Great Lakes and the St. Lawrence Seaway. It connects the past to the present. And finally it connects us to ourselves. On any given day along the river a hiker might meet people such as: Irene Best, who at age 80 still puts her kayak into the river; John Nasko, the artist who sketches river scenes from a canoe he built himself; Susan Urbas, a rower who for four years now has organized the Iron Oars Marathon, the longest smooth-water rowing race in the world; and many other fascinating people who enthusiastically enjoy together the many rewards of this walk. They are all very friendly. Your walk could take an extra hour, or perhaps days."

Four section maps provide interpretive material and show a preferred route along 30 miles of urban waterways. Maps are available from: Friends of the Chicago River, 53 W. Jackson, Suite 1135, Chicago, IL 60604. The maps are free, but a $2 fee is charged to cover postage. Checks should be made payable to: Friends of the Chicago River.

NORTHEASTERN ILLINOIS

Frank Lloyd Wright's Oak Park (11)

Directions: Oak Park is 10 miles west of downtown Chicago. Take the Eisenhower Expressway (I-290) to Harlem Avenue (Route 43) and exit north. Follow the brown-and-white signs to historic district parking at Forest Avenue and Lake Street.

Best Season: Year-round, but it's best on a sunny day.

Length: Allow at least half a day.

Degree of Difficulty: Easy.

Highlights: The world's largest collection of the architecture of Frank Lloyd Wright.

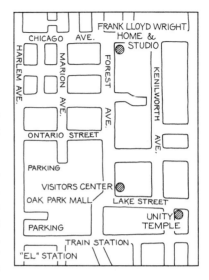

"I live here," says nominator Marylee Lyndall, "so I'm prejudiced, but this is a great tour. It's impossible not to be overwhelmed by the genius of Frank Lloyd Wright. Some of these houses are nearly 100 years old, but even today they look shockingly modern."

Between 1889 and 1909, Wright built twenty-five buildings in Oak Park, including Unity Temple, considered by some to be his masterpiece, and his own home and studio. It was during this time that Wright developed his early signature style, the Prairie house. These long, low dwellings virtually changed the course of twentieth-century American architecture.

During the week, this walk begins at the Visitors Center at 158 Forest Avenue. On the weekends, the tour departs from Wright's Home and Studio at 951 Chicago Avenue, at noon, or from Unity Temple, 875 Lake Street, at 2 p.m. Tickets may be purchased at the Visitors Center or at the Ginkgo Tree Bookshop, 951 Chicago Avenue. There is a $7 general admission charge; $4 for those aged 10 to 18 and over 65. Children under 10 are admitted free.

The tour is divided into three parts: Home and Studio, Unity Temple, and Historic District. Cassettes are available, but Marylee says "Don't settle for a recorded tour. Let an expert give you a personal introduction to Wright. You never know who you'll get, but they're more fun. These are people who love Frank Lloyd Wright's work and tell you their favorite stories." For more information regarding tour hours or special warm-weather walking tours, write the Oak Park Tour Center, 951 Chicago Avenue, Oak Park, IL 60302, or call (312) 848-1500.

SOUTHWESTERN ILLINOIS

Collinsville Walking Workout (12)

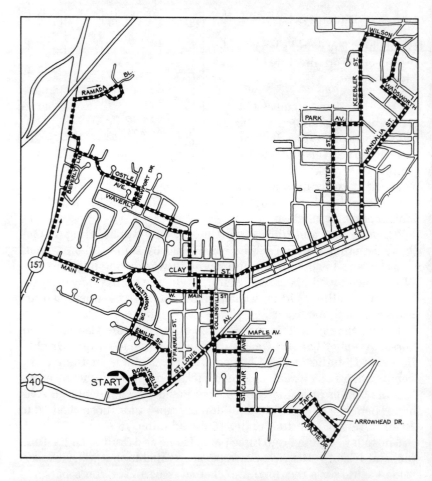

Directions: Collinsville is located across the Mississippi River from St. Louis, Missouri. Take I-70 to I-55 in Illinois and exit at Collinsville. This walk begins on Bosky Dells.

Best Season: Year-round, but you need to watch the weather for ice and snow in winter, which would make the hills rough going.

Length: 11.9 miles; allow about three or four hours for a brisk walking workout.

Degree of Difficulty: Moderately difficult to difficult.

Highlights: A real walking workout with plenty to see, including a fabulous view of St. Louis.

"The challenges of this route are what I enjoy most," says nominator Janet Delkus. The reason for the challenges are the several hills you'll go up and down on the walk. The first hill is Arrowhead, a small one to warm you up for the big ones to come. Ostle Hill is the toughest, but there's a great view at the top which is just the right reward. It's important to remember the need for deeper breathing to make it up the hills when you take this walk in the winter, Janet cautions. "It gets very cold and windy on the bluffs."

Ramada Hill presents less of a workout than Ostle Hill, Janet tells us, but the reward as you start the descent is even greater, for from here you'll get a one-of-a-kind view of St. Louis. Janet especially recommends taking this walk in the early morning or at sunset when this view is especially exquisite. "The arch is extraordinary, she says, "truly the gateway to the West."

Collinsville, which was incorporated in 1850 and began as a mining town, is now a growing, friendly city. As you wander through the streets of the downtown section, you'll find lots of smiles and friendly greetings. Just follow Janet's map, get a workout, and enjoy the sights in Collinsville. "There are so many interesting things to see on this walk," Janet says, "that your body gets a workout without ever feeling tired." She adds, "My home is on Bosky Dells. Please stop by and say hello. I will be happy to talk with anyone who wants to take this route. And maybe I'll join you."

West of the city, in E. St. Louis, you won't want to miss the Cahokia Mounds State Historic Site. Here there are ruins of the largest pre-Columbian community in the entire Mississippi River Valley.

WEST CENTRAL ILLINOIS

Red Oak Backpack Trail (13)

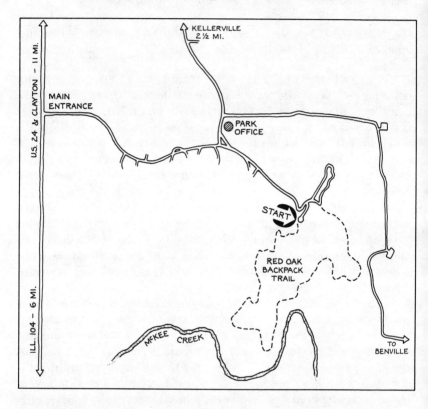

Directions: The trail is located in Siloam Springs State Park, about 25 miles east of Quincy. Take Route 104 from Quincy and watch for signs to the park.

Best Season: Year-round.

Length: 6 miles. There's lots to do, including boating and fishing, so you may want to make a full day of it.

Degree of Difficulty: Moderate.

Highlights: A wonderfully diverse walk that leads past a lake, across a dam, up and down hills, across a prairie, and along rocky ridges and gently flowing streams.

The best place to start this walk, according to Dave Copeland, who submitted it, is at the concession stand "because you can meet and visit with Bob, the concessionaire. Bob will share his collection of old photos of the park with the sincerely interested walker, including some shots of the 'old stone house,' which you'll see out on the trail."

Siloam Springs State Park encompasses 3,318 acres of rough glaciated terrain with deep ravines and narrow ridge tops as well as a 58-acre lake that Dave says "looks like it belongs in a storybook." The lake is stocked with largemouth bass, channel catfish, and rainbow trout, and fishing is permitted. A salmon stamp is required and may be purchased at the concession stand. Only sport fishing tackle may be used. Canoes, rowboats, and paddleboats are also available in the concession area, and there are two campgrounds and several picnic areas in the park.

The name *Siloam* is believed to have come from the biblical pool of Siloam where a blind man's sight was restored after he washed in the water. The springs here were named by their discoverer, Rev. Reuben K. McCoy, a Presbyterian minister from nearby Clayton, and were long believed to have "curative value."

The trail affords a wonderful opportunity to see a variety of interesting plant and animal life. Wildflowers, including wild rose, partridge pea, black-eyed Susan, white false indigo, and snapdragons, bloom all along the path, and the animals you might come across include quail, rabbit, fox, squirrel, raccoon, opossum, beaver, coyote, and deer. Overhead or in the shrubs, you might spot goldfinch, turkey vultures, hawks, eagles, woodpeckers, hummingbirds, whippoorwill, and wild turkey, to name just a few of the birds that can be seen in the area.

"I have hiked the trails of this park in all seasons," Dave says, "and I have never failed to see and enjoy the hilltop views, the babbling streams, and the always-present signs of wildlife; the sound of the wind in the trees unobstructed by city noises, the sound of an eagle in a nearby tree, the sight of a deer standing in the trail. I could possibly write a book about the good times I have had hiking and camping in this park, and I hope you will come out and enjoy it with me."

Indiana

SOUTHERN INDIANA

Two Lakes Trail (14)

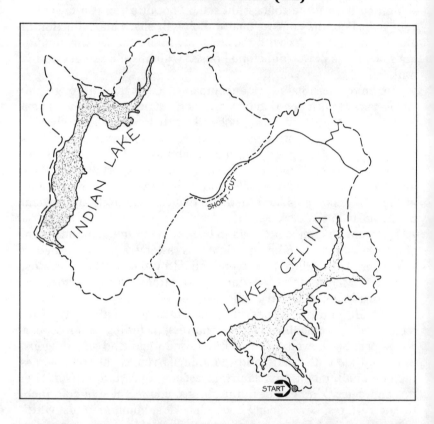

Directions: The trail is located in the Hoosier National Forest, between Evansville, Indiana, and Louisville, Kentucky. From I-64 take Route 37 south for 2 miles, and follow Forest Service signs to the forest.

Best Season: Spring, fall, winter.

Length: 12.2 miles; allow six to eight hours.

Degree of Difficulty: Easy to moderate.

Highlights: Panoramic lake views and peaceful strolls through the forest.

Two Lakes Trail, named for Indian Lake and Lake Celina, the two 140-acre lakes it encircles, provides a wonderful opportunity to feel at one with nature. It winds leisurely through the forest where, if you're quiet, you may spot wild turkey or deer or any of the wide variety of wildlife who live there. Spring is particularly beautiful because the wildflowers and flowering trees such as dogwood are in bloom, and mushroom hunting is good along the trail. Fall is spectacular with the rich colors of orange, gold, red, and yellow. But nominator David Kissel likes the trail best in winter, "when you can get better views of the lakes, rock outcrops, and rolling hills."

Because it is part of a national forest, the fish, plant, and wildlife in the area are carefully monitored to ensure preservation of the ecological balance. Originally established to protect watersheds and supply timber, today national forest land throughout the country also provides recreation opportunities for the public such as hiking, fishing, camping, and boating. For further information about the range of activities available in this forest, write: Hoosier National Forest, 811 Constitution Avenue, Bedford, IN 47421.

Not far from the Two Lakes Trail and Hoosier National Forest is the Wyandotte Cave, the largest cave in the United States and one of the most important. If you would like to visit this historic site, get back on I-64 and head east to Wyandotte. Follow signs to the cave, where you can walk through some 25 miles of passageways, view the largest underground mountain in the country (140 feet high) and stand in the biggest underground room.

SOUTHERN INDIANA

Knobstone Trail (15)

Directions: This walk begins in Deam Lake State Recreation Area. From Louisville, Kentucky, take I-65 north approximately 8 miles to Route 60. Go west on Route 60 for about 9 miles to Deam Lake State Recreation Area. Follow signs to the Deam Lake Trailhead.

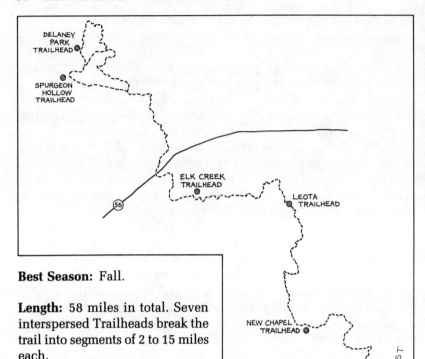

Best Season: Fall.

Length: 58 miles in total. Seven interspersed Trailheads break the trail into segments of 2 to 15 miles each.

Degree of Difficulty: Moderately difficult.

Highlights: Breathtaking vistas from overlooks; cool stream valleys, a profusion of wildflowers and wildlife, and exceptional autumn foliage.

This scenic trail is the longest footpath in Indiana and traverses some of the state's most beautiful and rugged land. Named for the "knobstone" shale which is common to the area, the trail follows the Knobstone Escarpment, which is mostly hardwood forest. In places the escarpment rises to more than 300 feet above the low-lying farmland, offering wonderful views of the surrounding land.

The Indiana Department of Natural Resources, which manages the trail, plans to extend the Knobstone Trail from its present length of 58 miles to 100 miles. You can actually get on the trail at a number of different points, and, of course, it's not necessary to hike the entire 58 miles. For example, if you enter the trail at the Deam Lake Trailhead as suggested here, you can walk to the Jackson Road Trailhead, a distance of 5 miles. The trail parallels the shore of Deam Lake, crosses over moderately rolling terrain, and traverses two very steep slopes. From the Jackson Road Trailhead, you can continue on for another 12 or so miles to the New Chapel Trailhead, or you can head back to your car at Deam Lake for a total distance of 10 miles round-trip. If you decide to continue your walk, the scenery from the Jackson Road Trailhead to the New Chapel Trailhead includes an overlook from which you can see (on a clear day) the city of Louisville, Kentucky. This part of the trail crosses several small streams and goes over rolling terrain, climbing up ridgetops, and then dropping about 300 feet. For further information on the various trail segments, write the Indiana Department of Natural Resources, 605 State Office Building, Indianapolis, IN 46204, or call them at (317) 232-4070.

The Knobstone Trail is well marked with "KT" posts and information signs at the Trailheads and 2 × 6 inch white trail blazes on trees along the way. Two blazes indicate a change in direction, and the hiker should locate the next blaze before continuing. Most of the streams along the trail are dry for a good part of the year, and so hikers should carry their own water.

There are facilities at the Deam Lake Recreation Area for boating, swimming, camping, and picnicking. Stop at the gatehouse, 1¼ miles west of the Trailhead, for more information.

Nominator Paul Sherwood suggests you plan to hike the trail in the fall when there is a glorious display of foliage.

NORTH CENTRAL INDIANA

East Race Waterway Walk (16)

Directions: The walk follows the East Race Waterway in South Bend. Take the 80/90 Toll Road to Route 33 and head south to La Salle Avenue. Drive east for four blocks.

Best Season: Spring, summer, fall.

Length: 3 to 5 miles.

Degree of Difficulty: Easy; no steep hills, paved walkway.

Highlights: A chance to "get away from it all" while remaining right in the city.

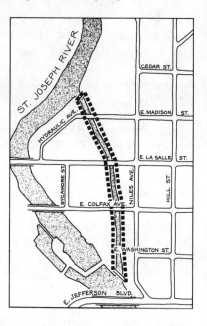

This walk follows the East Race Waterway, the only artificially created white water rapids in North America. Nominators Sandy Poulos and Bill Wight say it provides "beautiful river scenery right in the heart of a bustling city."

The Race Waterway was constructed in the 1840s as a channel off the St. Joseph River to provide power to industry in South Bend. The St. Joseph River runs from Klinger Lake in Michigan down into Indiana, where it takes a big bend (thus "South Bend") before heading north to empty into Lake Michigan. It was from this river that La Salle, in 1679, first saw what we now call Indiana and was impressed by the beauty of its "prairies, streams, rivers, fish and game." In the summer you can cross a footbridge over the White Water Rapids and picnic on the river at Island Park.

The Race Waterway almost disappeared because in the 1920s electricity replaced hydraulic power and in the 1960s and 1970s builders began filling in the waterway with rubble and debris. Finally, in the early 1980s, the waterway received a new lease on life when the city of South Bend decided to make it a recreational area. It was redug, and the bottom and sides were covered with cement. Completed in 1984 at a total cost of $4.6 million, it now provides a beautiful natural environment in the middle of the city and is home to national and international kayak competitions. It is also open at various times for recreational canoeing and inner tubing.

The walkway makes a loop down one side of the waterway and up the other. It is lined with trees and shared by joggers, walkers, and bicyclists. At several places pedestrian bridges cross over the waterway, and sometimes the walk takes you right under the city streets. "You'll meet lots of interesting people," says Sandy Poulos, "and enjoy beautiful scenery." Sandy especially likes to take this walk at dusk when it is particularly "therapeutic."

For more information on the East Race Waterway, call the South Bend Convention and Tourism Division at (219) 234-0079.

CENTRAL INDIANA

Historic Plainfield (17)

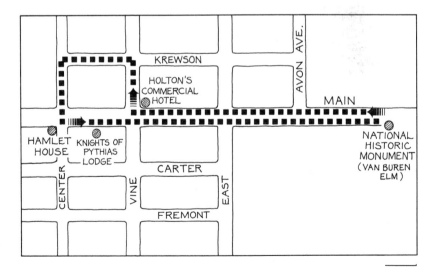

Directions: Plainfield is located just 14 miles west of Indianapolis on State Route 40, about 2 miles north of I-70. The walk begins at the Van Buren Elm marker on the lawn of the Western Yearly Meeting House of the Friends on East Main Street.

Best Season: Spring, summer, fall.

Length: 1 mile; allow one to two hours.

Degree of Difficulty: Easy.

Highlights: A tour through a town of Quaker origin whose Main Street is part of the "most famous road in America."

Plainfield's roots are Quaker, and this heritage is celebrated every year when Quakers from all over the country continue a tradition that began in 1858 by attending their annual meeting at the Plainfield Western Yearly Meeting of Friends Meeting House. This walk begins on the lawn of the Meeting House at the stone which marks the location of the Van Buren Elm, another historic Plainfield site.

The story behind President Martin Van Buren and the town of Plainfield, Indiana, is unique. It actually begins long before Martin Van Buren was born, when George Washington, in an effort to make the frontier more hospitable, urged the creation of a road through the wilderness. Washington's dream became a reality known as the Old National Trails Road, linking Washington, D.C., with St. Louis, Missouri.

Everything went along fine on the road until 1830 when for a period of more than ten years what was to become a familiar problem arose: lack of federal funds. The road deteriorated until it was virtually impassable due to mudholes and tree roots. The roots of one particular tree became famous.

While Martin Van Buren was president, he vetoed a bill passed by Congress which would have appropriated money to fix the road. So, it was probably not surprising that, when on a visit to Plainfield in 1842, shortly after the end of his presidency, Van Buren was purposely "dumped" from his stagecoach at the foot of the giant elm tree whose roots jutted out into the road. (Stagecoaches were called "shake guts" at the time because of what happened to passengers due to the awful road.) Not long after the incident, there was money to repair the road!

This walk, nominated by Mary Miller and Jean Davis, begins at the Van Buren Elm site and goes west on Main Street to Vine. On the northeast corner of Vine and Main stands the former Holton's Commercial Hotel, once considered "the finest in Plainfield." From here, walk one block north and turn left on Krewson, then left again on Center Street. At the corner of Center and Main is Hamlet House, built on the site where Van Buren "recuperated" after the infamous stagecoach incident. In 1891, this building housed the Keeley Institute, a famous alcohol and drug-abuse treatment center. There are many Civil War era houses on Center Street which served as stations on the underground railroads.

As you head back on Main toward the Meeting House, you'll pass the old Knights of Pythias Lodge, which had a brief history as the Plainfield Opera House.

For a detailed map of Plainfield and more information on the town, contact Susan Carter, historical librarian at the Plainfield Library: (317) 839-6602.

CENTRAL INDIANA

Indianapolis Discovery Walk (18)

Directions: The walk begins at Union Station in downtown Indianapolis.

Best Season: Spring, fall, and summer.

Length: There is a lot to discover in Indianapolis; you may want to allot a whole day (and night, too).

Degree of Difficulty: Easy.

Highlights: The discoveries awaiting you in Indianapolis include a visit to the homes of poet James Whitcomb Riley and President Benjamin Harrison, as well as exciting Union Station, a "festival marketplace," and a Holiday Inn that's not to be missed!

"Indianapolis is experiencing a renaissance," says nominator Sue Goodell. "During the past ten years or so there's been a great emphasis placed on urban revitalization." A good example of this is the restoration project at the Union Station where this "discovery" walk begins. Located on the site of America's first union rail depot, the 750,000-square-foot structure was built in 1888, and while a few trains still pass through each day, the focus of Union Station is now on people. In addition to its many shops and restaurants, there's a museum called the Indiana Experience where a moving walkway, video theater, and several hands-on exhibits allow you to get into the spirit of the state. There's also a one-of-a-kind Holiday Inn which, in addition to its 276 rooms, has 26 suites which

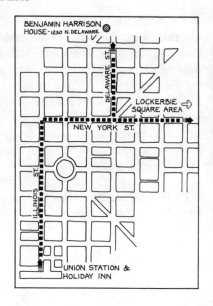

are old Pullman cars decorated along "celebrity" themes. "There's a homey Cole Porter suite," Sue explains, "and a Rudy Valentino suite done in leopard skin!"

From Union Station, Sue suggests you walk to nearby Lockerbie Square, a restored late-nineteenth-century area with old-fashioned lighting and cobblestone streets. At 528 Lockerbie Street, you can visit the home of poet James Whitcomb Riley, who lived in Indianapolis and died there in 1916. The home, which is considered by historians to be one of the most perfectly preserved Victorian homes in the United States, is open from 10 a.m. to 4 p.m. Tuesday through Saturday. Riley was an extremely popular American poet, perhaps because his down-home verses captured the "goodness" of America and Americans. Today his poems bring a feeling of nostalgia for simpler days of strawberry fields and "old swimmin' holes." In Riley's words: "O, it sets my heart a-clickin' like the tickin' of a clock, When the frost is on the punkin and the fodder's in the shock."

Riley's nickname of "Hoosier Poet" raises the question of the "Hoosier" mystery. "No one really knows how the state got that name," Sue says. Actually there are several theories—all unproven. One holds that when pioneers moved west and settled in Indiana, people already there would ask, "Who's yer?" ("Who are you?") A related theory holds that Hoosier comes from the way people used to answer a knock on the door, a version of "Who's there?" A third theory is that Samuel Hoosier, an Indiana canal builder, preferred to hire Indiana men, who thus earned the nickname Hoosiers. Whatever the reason, "Hoosier State" it is—and one of the most beautiful in the country.

North of Lockerbie Square at 1230 No. Delaware Street is the home of Benjamin Harrison, who lived there for fourteen years before becoming the twenty-third president of the United States. The 16-room Italianate mansion has a third-floor ballroom and original furnishings in many of the rooms (including Harrison's chair, which is made of cattle horns and has a plaque with Harrison's name spelled out in diamonds). The home is open from 10 a.m. to 4 p.m. Monday through Saturday and from 12:30 to 4 p.m. on Sundays.

Before you leave Indianapolis, Sue Goodell highly recommends you visit the Eagle Creek Park, one of the largest municipal parks in the country. It occupies 4,400 acres on the northwest side of the city and includes miles of walking paths, bike trails, a nature preserve, and a 1,300-acre reservoir for boating and swimming.

Indianapolis is also home to a brand-new 64-acre zoo which has the largest indoor whale and dolphin pavilion in the country. Located just six blocks from downtown hotels, the zoo is "cageless"; more than 2,000 animals live in simulated natural habitats. "It's not to be missed!" Sue tells us.

NORTHEASTERN INDIANA

Bixler Lake Park: Wetlands Trail (19)

Directions: The trail is located in Bixler Lake Park, Kendallville, Indiana. From Kendallville's Main Street, take Diamond Street west to Bixler Lake Park.

Best Season: Spring and fall.

Length: 3.1 miles.

Degree of Difficulty: Moderately easy.

Highlights: Seclusion and peaceful beauty just minutes from the downtown area.

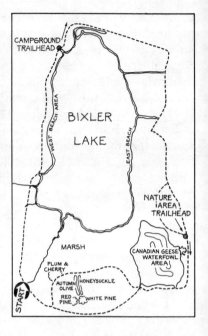

For nominator James Goodwin, Bixler Lake Park is a special "getaway" right within the city limits. The 117-acre lake is surrounded by a variety of parkland, including a hardwood forest (gorgeous in the fall, with bright red, yellow, and orange foliage), open fields, and wetlands which attract all sorts of migratory waterfowl. In the secluded areas of the park, watch for great horned owls, Canada geese, and whitetail deer. There are observation platforms which overlook the nesting sites of duck and geese. The Wetlands Trail runs through the wetlands and circles Bixler Lake, one of the few lakes in Indiana within city limits. Jim says it is especially beautiful in spring, when the wildflowers are in bloom, and in the fall, because of the foliage.

There are two shorter trails which are sections of the longer Wetlands Trail. One is 1.5 miles and runs through the campgrounds. "It's wonderful here in the evening," Jim says, "when the smells of nature mix with the aromas of fresh coffee and food cooking over the fire."

The second loop trail is 1.7 miles and leads through the nature area. According to Jim, this trail passes through the prettiest part of the woods and includes an overlook to nesting islands and a waterfowl resting area. It gives a nice flavor of the park, and is perfect for anyone who wants to see the wetlands, but can't walk the 3.1 miles around the lake.

There are informative signs along the trails, but to get the most out of your walk, pick up a free map and self-guiding tree identification booklet at the Wetlands Trail Trailhead.

Plan to stop at the beach for a while if you're in Bixler Park during the summer, and don't forget your cross-country skis in the winter. This place has a little something for everyone!

WEST CENTRAL INDIANA

Portland Arch Nature Preserve (20)

Directions: From Attica, go south on U.S. 41 for about 5 miles, then west on County Road 650N. Once in the village of Fountain, follow signs to the preserve. There are two parking lots, each with an adjoining self-guiding trail. The trail from the first parking lot leads to the arch. Portland Arch Nature Preserve is about 72 miles from Indianapolis. Take I-74 west to U.S. 41 and go north about 7 miles. Turn west on County Road 650N to Fountain.

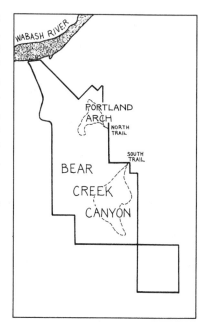

Best Season: Year-round.

Length: There are two trails of 1 mile each.

Degree of Difficulty: Easy.

Highlights: Eastern white pines hug the steep sandstone cliffs in this very scenic area.

This is a special area because it is filled with plants that are endangered in the state, such as white pines, Canada blueberry, and the bush honeysuckle. Nature preserves (there are 107 of them in Indiana) are considered so important and so sensitive that they do not appear on state maps. Be careful during your walk here and remember that fires and camping are prohibited as is rock climbing which is extremely dangerous.

There are 253 acres in the preserve, and the two mile-long trails are self-guided with lots of information along the routes. On one of the trails, you'll pass under the branches of sugar maples, white pines, and oaks, then descend a steep slope to Portland Arch, a natural stone arch created by a small tributary to Bear Creek, which over the years cut into the sandstone bluff. Here you'll find an enormous variety of plant life, including examples of the lower plant kingdom: mosses, ferns, and liverworts, as well as scattered beds of blueberry, huckleberry and wintergreen. Look for the Canada blueberry; this is the only place in the state where it is found. Along the other trail, you'll explore the history of the area and the various stages of the preserve.

Bear Creek Canyon is spectacular; vertical sandstone cliffs rise over 100 feet, and trees—hardwoods and white pines—miraculously poke out of the rock wall.

Following your visit to the nature preserve, we suggest a drive south on Route 41 to Turkey Run State Park, about 25 miles from Fountain. The park, in the valley of Sugar Creek, was named for the wild turkeys that used to live here. It is a magnificent place with awesome sandstone cliffs and 14 miles of trails which allow you to explore the Turkey Run canyons up close. As you walk these trails, you should be aware that you are walking in the footsteps of the Miami Indians who were here some 300 years before you. You'll see a museum in the park, a church, and two covered bridges. To give yourself enough time in this beautiful place, you may want to spend the night at the Turkey Run Inn.

From the park, you can take Route 47 north to I-74, then head east back to Indianapolis.

NORTHWESTERN INDIANA

Indiana Dunes (21)

Directions: From Chicago, take I-94 to Chesterton, Indiana (Highway 49). Head north for 2 miles to the entrance of the park. The walk begins at the Nature Center.

Best Season: Year-round.

Length: The trail is about 5 miles, but it can take about three hours because there are so many nice places to stop.

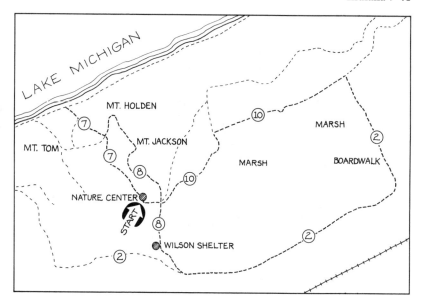

Degree of Difficulty: Easy to moderate.

Highlights: A trail through forests and along the beach. Many who have taken it call it their favorite trail.

There are 27 miles of trail among the 2,182 acres of Indiana Dunes State Park, 3 miles along the shore of Lake Michigan. The area is unique and includes an amazing diversity of plant and wildlife. It is one of the only places in the country where you can find dogwood along with tundra bearberries and prairie wildflowers growing near cacti. The dunes are a result of a steady northwesterly wind blowing the sand up from the beach. When vegetation took hold, it blocked the wind so that the sand accumulated.

Those who have hiked in Indiana Dunes enthusiastically recommend all the trails. "I have had many wonderful experiences here," says one long-time Indiana Dunes hiker. "It's only an hour from Chicago, so every time I have visitors who have never been to Chicago, I give them a day at the Dunes. They always love it. I've taken people from Germany, England, Canada, India, and all over the United States, and even though I promise them the most wonderful day of their lives, they are never disappointed."

One of the favorite routes begins at the Nature Center on Trail 10 and turns off on Trail 2, across the Boardwalk which leads over the marsh. From here, head back to the Wilson Shelter area. Then take Trail 8 to Trail 7, back past the Nature Center. Stay on Trail 7 to the beach, and then walk back to the Nature Center where you can stop for a while to watch the birds and animals.

The scenery changes dramatically throughout this hike, which begins in the woods, goes through a marsh, then back through the woods, and over the dunes. At that point, you turn a corner and get a breathtaking view of the beach, Lake Michigan, and (on a clear day) the Chicago skyline on the horizon. You can climb down the dune and walk along the beach as far as you want to go. (If you parked at the Nature Center, your car is only twenty minutes away).

Swimming is permitted in Lake Michigan during the summer (as long as there is a lifeguard on duty). There are also lots of picnic and camping areas. If you're hungry or cold after your hike, stop in at Winfield's piano bar on Highway 49, about 2½ miles south of the park.

Iowa

NORTHWESTERN IOWA

Puddle-Jumper Trail (22)

Directions: The Puddle-Jumper Trail is between Alton and Orange City. Enter Orange City from the east on State Highway 10. Turn left on County Road 64 and go about two blocks to the western end of the trail. There's a parking lot across the street from the Northwestern College athletic field.

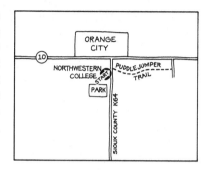

Best Season: Year-round; in fall, wild prairie asters, goldenrod, and sunflowers are in bloom; in summer, the fragrant wild roses.

Length: 4 miles round-trip.

Degree of Difficulty: Easy.

Highlights: A refuge for birds and animals, the trail preserves an original prairie habitat.

We have no statistics to show just how many old railroad beds have become popular walking trails, but we know there are a lot of them, and we think it's a wonderful way to recycle!

The Puddle-Jumper Trail, on a former bed of the Chicago & Northwestern Railroad is a favorite of Doris Vogel, who says, "There's nothing better than a vigorous walk on the Puddle-Jumper!"

The name *Iowa* comes from an Indian word meaning "beautiful land," and the Puddle-Jumper gives you a chance to see some of this beautiful land up close. Freshly disked, meticulously kept farm fields stretch out on either side, giving off an earthy musk aroma, and along the trail itself, signs identify the varieties of plants, shrubs, trees, and grasses. More than 200 native and 17 woodland plants have been identified. "Remarkable," points out Doris, considering the damage humankind has inflicted on the area with herbicides, cinder dumping, etc. "A glance at the vegetation map," she says, "reveals many interesting species already planted or to be planted in time to come: cherry trees, black walnut, Russian olives, Colorado blue spruce, white pine, ginkgo, yucca, sumacs, sweet william, day lilies, river birch, locusts, chokecherries, buffalo and blue grasses, and many, many others."

The path, composed of packed, crushed quartzite, makes for comfortable walking, and fitness stations are spaced along the way for those interested in a workout. Restored bridges cross over little gullies, and a rest stop along the way has play equipment for children. But the big surprise is—buffalo!! "They're kept by a local businessman," explains Doris, "but their ancestors probably roamed this very area."

On the return trip, Doris suggests you might want to "walk down in the ditch in the cottonwood trail to flush out a pheasant or a quail or a rabbit." Walking back to your car, you'll see the big Orange City orange ball water tower, the windmill arms of the Orange City Windmill Bank, the courthouse tower, and the pink-brick buildings of Northwestern College.

"The trail can be used for cross-country skiing in the winter," Doris says, "but in every season the changing scene affords its peculiar delights to the walking enthusiast."

NORTHEASTERN IOWA

Heritage Trail (23)

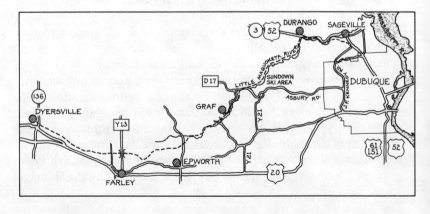

Directions: Take U.S. 52 north of Dubuque. The parking lot for Heritage Trail is marked at Durango, about 2 miles north of Dubuque. There's a $1 per day fee for everyone aged 12 to 64.

Best Season: Spring and fall, though the trail is open year-round and is sheltered by the valley in the winter.

Length: Heritage Trail is 26 miles long. This section is 16 miles round-trip. Allow about six hours.

Degree of Difficulty: Easy. The trail is at least eight feet wide and has less than a 1 percent grade. Stay on the path; nettles, poison ivy, and poison parsnip are the reward for those who don't!

Highlights: Feel a part of history as you follow an old railbed along the scenic Little Maquoketa River.

Nominator Doug Cheever tells us that the Heritage Trail is special because it combines "beautiful scenery, natural history, geologic formations, and archaeology." Sixteen points of interest are marked along the 8-mile length nominated, and a guidebook is available.

The trail follows an old Chicago Great Western Railroad bed along the Little Maquoketa River through a deep valley bordered by sheer limestone cliffs, 450 feet high. It can get pretty crowded in the fall, warns Doug, because bicyclists and walkers come from all over to enjoy the fabulous fall colors. (That should tell you something!)

The area is significant from an historical standpoint because it is part of what is known as the "driftless area," a section of land not continuously covered with ice during glacial periods. Here plant and animal species found refuge until the glaciers retreated. Some of these species remain, now separated by hundreds of miles from their nearest relatives.

Animal and plant life were again threatened when the settlers arrived and changed the natural surroundings of the prairie states. In Iowa, elk were hunted out by the 1860s, black bear by the 1880s, and deer, beaver, otter, wolves, and mountain lion soon after. As you walk along the Heritage Trail, you will, perhaps, be more aware of the significance of the surrounding woodland if you remember that in the first 100 years of settlement, half the woodland area in Dubuque County was cleared and 99.9 percent of the prairie plowed. Now that

we have become more conscious of the effects of such drastic ecological change, not only on the plant and animals species who used
to live here, but also on ourselves, and have begun to make concerted
efforts to regain some of what we have lost, some of the species—
deer and beaver, for example—are making a comeback.

Europeans first came to this part of Iowa in 1788 when Julien
Dubuque, a French Canadian, settled here to exploit the lead mines.
The city named for him is the oldest in Iowa and the old river town
is worth a visit in its own right. If you have time, take the Fourth
Street cable car from Cable Car Square to Fenelon Place, which is at
the top of a bluff overlooking the Mississippi River.

The lead mines near Durango along the Little Maquoketa River
are some of the oldest in the area, apparently mined by the Indians
even before the arrival of the white settlers. The lovely curved bridge
that crosses the Little Maquoketa River in Durango was built in 1915
and is 210 feet long. The backdrop of sheer rock bluffs makes this
bridge a favorite for photographers.

For the adventuresome, there's a canoe launch site at Durango from
which you can take an 8-mile trip to the Mississippi.

EAST CENTRAL IOWA

Cedar Valley Nature Trail (24)

Directions: Take I-380 to north Cedar Rapids and exit on Boyson
Road. The Trailhead is about a quarter mile east of the exit.

Best Season: Spring, but the trail is open year-round, and nominator Alice Anderson, who likes to cross-country ski, says, "Winter is
definitely my favorite time."

Length: 53 miles, one way.

Degree of Difficulty: Easy, but due to the length of the trail, walkers
should be aware of the fatigue factor and plan ahead. (There are
plenty of restaurants, picnic grounds, camping areas, and places to
stay the night along the route.) Stop often to rest, and carry plenty of
water on hot days.

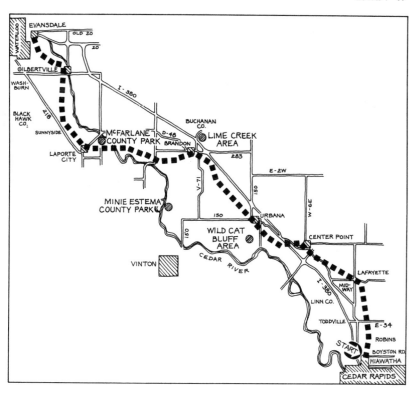

Highlights: According to Alice Anderson, this is "the most outstanding trail in Iowa!" Highlights include historical landmarks, archaeological sites, wildlife, farms, and small towns.

This 53-mile trail is the longest one in the region, linking two metropolitan areas (Cedar Rapids and Waterloo). Constructed on a portion of the former Illinois Gulf Railroad, the trail provides an unparalleled opportunity to walk for miles and miles through incredibly varying landscapes and vistas. The route passes alongside the banks of the Cedar River, through lush, rolling farmlands and numerous small towns. Keep an eye out for deer, badger, and wild turkey, and, if you're walking the trail in spring, you'll see an abundance of colorful wildflowers.

Walkers can appreciate the importance of this former railroad by making a stop at the restored depot located at Gilbertville. There are various historical landmarks all along the trail, and another depot, located at Center Point, is currently under renovation and will be a railroad museum.

Take a little time to plan this walk. There are many restaurants in the small towns you'll pass through, as well as motels, hotels, and bed-and-breakfast inns. In addition, there are nearby recreation areas and campgrounds for boating, fishing, picnicking, and camping. For more information, write to Linn County Conservation Board, 1890 County Home Road, Marion, IA 52302, telephone number: (319) 398-3505, or the Black Hawk County Conservation Board, 2410 W. Lone Tree Road, Cedar Falls, IA 50613; telephone number: (319) 266-0328.

Before or after your walk, you'll want to take time to explore the city of Cedar Rapids, with its seventy-three parks. One of the loveliest is Bever Park, off 19th Street, S.E., on Bever Avenue. On the southwest quadrant of the city between 15th and 16th avenues is the Czech Village, a fascinating historical area. Brucemore Mansion and Estate, now a community cultural center, is open for tours from February through December by appointment. Call (319) 362-7375. Visitors can explore the 26-acre estate of formal gardens and the twenty-one room Queen Anne–style mansion.

CENTRAL IOWA

Three Walks in Des Moines (25)

Directions: Take I-80 or I-35 to I-235 and exit at Seventh Street. The first walk begins at the Locust Street Mall in the Skywalk System.

Best Season: The Skywalk Golf Tournament is held in February, but you can walk the Skywalk year-round. Des Moines is at its best from spring through fall, but for the two outdoor walks, any nice day is great.

Length: The golf tournament covers a portion of the 2½ mile Skywalk. Allow about an hour. The Journey walk through an historic residential area of Des Moines is about 1½ miles; the Two Rivers Volkswalk is 10 kilometers (6.2miles).

Degree of Difficulty: Easy. Even the Two Rivers walk follows mostly city sidewalks or flat bike paths.

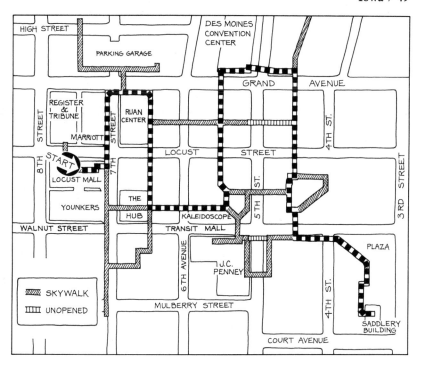

Highlights: Each of these walks gives you a chance to see Des Moines from a different perspective. One is just plain fun, one is informative, one is invigorating. Plan to walk all three!

Des Moines' Skywalk Golf Tournament

This unique walk—a golf tournament under glass—was nominated by Barbara Lovitt. It takes place annually in February, when the Skywalk of downtown Des Moines is turned into a fairway. A "secret" handicap system is used to compile the scores, so that novice golfers as well as "pros" have a chance to win the all-par-three Skywalk Open. Even if you just watch, this special day is enormous fun for the whole family. You'll have a chance to meet enthusiastic people (about 1,100 of them) who enjoy "putting," window shopping, and good food. The only hazard, Barbara cautions, may be "getting hit in the ankle by a stray putt-putt golf ball!"

If you can't make it to the Sky-walk Open, Barbara encourages you to plan a walk through the climate-controlled Skywalk any time of year. It's a great way to see the city.

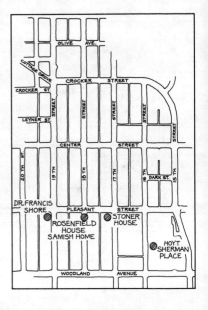

The Journey

The Journey is a 1½-mile tour of the historic Sherman Hill district of Des Moines, one of the first res-idential areas to be built in the city. Pick up a self-guided tour bro-chure at the Convention and Vis-itors Bureau Information Center in the Kaleidoscope, downtown.

The district gets its name from Hoyt Sherman, a Des Moines post-master, who bought five acres of a huge estate and built his home in 1877 at 15th Street and Woodland Avenue. Today the Sherman home is the first stop on this Journey. Inside you'll find additions of an art gallery and an auditorium, as well as Sherman's original home.

The Journey takes you past several fascinating examples of turn-of-the-century architecture, including the home of Dr. Francis Shore, which was built in 1895 for $2,000! As you walk past these fine old homes, you will gain an appreciation for the various influences on the architecture of the period. You'll recognize the European influ-ence, for example, in the Stoner House, located at 692 17th Street. Built in 1893 in the French "chateauesque" style, it features steep roofs, gables, and a corner tower. The Rosenfield House at 696 18th Street and the Samish Home across the street are examples of the transition between Victorian architecture and architecture with roots that go back to America's colonial past. This transition eventually resulted in the Colonial Revival period.

Two Rivers Volkswalk

From Skywalk to historic walk to volkswalk, Des Moines is truly a walker's city. The American Volkssport Association has sanctioned

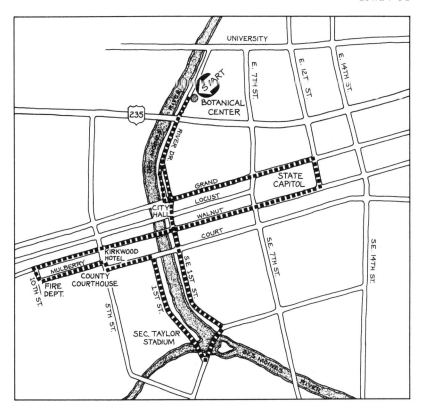

Two Rivers Walk as a year-round, noncompetitive, 10-kilometer walk through the city. Nominator Chris Larson tells us that the route is clearly marked and that everyone who walks it receives a map indicating points of interest along the way. All who complete the Two Rivers Walk receive an event award.

The Two Rivers Volkswalk begins at the Des Moines Botanical Center at 909 River Drive. Follow the metal signs past various city buildings and monuments to Ft. Des Moines, established in 1842 by Captain James Allen after the signing of a treaty with the Sac and Fox Indians. The walk then loops back to finish where it started—at the Botanical Center. The center is definitely worth a visit: It houses more than 15,000 plants and an award-winning bonsai collection.

Kansas

NORTHERN KANSAS

South Solomon River Trail (26)

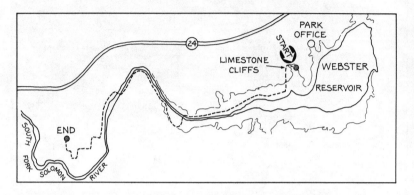

Directions: Located in Webster State Park, 8 miles west of Stockton, the Trailhead can be reached via Route 24.

Best Season: Spring and fall. (Trail is closed the first two weeks in December for Firearm Deer Season.)

Length: 10 miles one way; allow about five hours and arrange to have two cars, one at either end of the trail, if possible.

Degree of Difficulty: Easy.

Highlights: An isolated journey through varied terrain.

Webster Lake was built for flood control and irrigation by the Bureau of Land Control, but it resulted in an added benefit for those of us who enjoy walking. The 10-mile South Solomon River Trail follows the north shore of the Webster Reservoir and South Solomon River. The trail is marked by three-foot-high markers (hard to see in summer when the rich vegetation takes over), as well as by blue trail blazes on trees. It begins by passing through limestone cliffs and then follows the lake shoreline along sandy paths. Cottonwood and mulberry bushes alternate with short grasses, cactus, and sand hills to provide an ever-changing landscape. "Don't be surprised," says nominator Don Jenkins, Jr., "if a friendly deer accompanies you along the trail." You may also see wild turkey or even a bobcat or raccoon. Look for beaver, too. But even if you miss them, you are sure to see their dams.

The trail crosses the river at two points, so be sure you take this walk at a time when you can wade across (spring and fall). Of course, you can hike partway any time of year.

There are five campsites in the park, but no drinking water, so bring provisions. It can be extremely hot in summer (100°F at times), so water is important.

About 10 miles west of the park is the historic town of Nicodemus. Kansas became a state in 1861 just as the nation was about to become embroiled in the Civil War, and as a "free state," she quickly became a refuge for runaway slaves. Nicodemus was founded in 1877 by former slaves from Kentucky. Today it is a national historic landmark.

SOUTHWESTERN KANSAS

Cimarron National Grassland (27)

Directions: The Cimarron National Grassland is located in the extreme southwest corner of Kansas. Take Highway 27 or 56 to Elkhart and stop at headquarters for information.

Best Season: Year-round.

Length: There are many miles of primitive roads to walk, so plan to spend at least half a day here.

Degree of Difficulty: Easy.

Highlights: Follow the Cimarron River to your heart's content, or walk the historic Sante Fe Trail.

The Cimarron National Grassland covers about 108,000 acres, and while there are no specifically marked hiking trails, except the grass-covered Sante Fe Trail, miles of primitive roads follow the Cimarron River and provide hours of walking pleasure. Nancy Burton, who nominated the walk, says, "You can't get lost because it's so wide open that you can always see where you are going."

A 22-mile portion of the historic Sante Fe Trail passes through the grassland and is marked by mile-distant signs. "The signs help to see it," Nancy explains, "because most of the trail has been covered up by the grasses—buffalo grass, blue gama grass, bluestem, and Indian grass have all grown up over the trail." These grasses grow no higher than knee-deep, so it's easy and fun to walk in them.

It is hard to imagine when you see the grass-covered trail that in the 1800s, wagon trains made the forty- to sixty-day trip over the trail from Independence, Missouri, to Santa Fe, New Mexico. They would travel six abreast in the open areas to break the wind. The trail through Kansas had its birthplace in Council Grove in the heart of the Flint Hills, about 300 miles northeast of Elkhart. There, in 1825, the Osage Indians signed a treaty with the U.S. government which permitted the trail's passage through Indian land. Fifty-five years later, the Santa Fe Railroad reached Santa Fe, and the trail—almost overnight—was no longer used.

Today the largest portion of public access to the old Santa Fe Trail is in Cimarron National Grassland where it follows the course of the Cimarron River, never farther than 1 to 2 miles from it. The river is often dry, but it fills up after the heavy rains in spring and summer. The rain brings out the wildflowers, too, and you'll pass by yucca and sagebrush on your walk. Wildlife—deer, for example, and elk—can be seen in the evenings or before sunrise. During the hot days, they stay under shady cover.

SOUTHEASTERN KANSAS

Elk River Hiking Trail (28)

Directions: The trail is 7 miles northwest of Independence. Take Highway 160 from Independence and follow signs to Elk City Lake. Cross the Elk City Lake Dam and head north for ¼ mile. Turn left

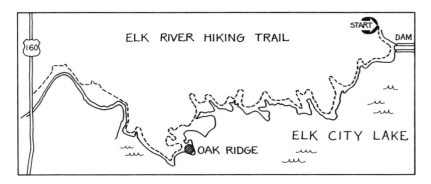

toward the brick building and parking lot which is the eastern Trailhead of the Elk River Trail.

Best Season: Spring and fall.

Length: 15 miles, but there are four places where you can turn off the trail if you want a shorter walk.

Degree of Difficulty: Moderately difficult. This is one of the most rugged trails in Kansas.

Highlights: Birds, wildlife, a variety of plant life, beautiful lake views, and dramatic topography make this one of the best trails in Kansas.

This one is a surprise; you just don't expect to see such dramatic terrain in Kansas. The trail begins near a stream crossing and then rises straight up the limestone bluffs to about 900 feet above sea level. Nominator Eugene Goff suggests you wear good hiking boots because this part of the trail is rugged. You may also want to pack a lunch as there are numerous overlooks where you can stop and enjoy the view.

From here the scene changes to prairie, and native grasses of big blue and little bluestem grow at least knee-high alongside the path. The rest of the trail alternates between wooded areas with hickory, oak, redbud, and walnut trees and more open areas. Eugene loves "the neat views of the lake," which you see most of the time as the trail follows the northwestern shoreline. He prefers to hike the trail in the fall when the colors are spectacular and the leaves crunch softly underfoot, but he says spring is also nice because the wildflowers are everywhere.

An occasional waterfall adds to the scenic beauty of the place, and it is possible to see quail, white-tailed deer, rabbit, squirrel, wild turkey, bobcat, coyote, and beaver. In the winter, you can spot bald eagles, if you're lucky, and you're sure to see geese, herons, and ducks. On the less inspiring side, you may also see a scorpion or two and an occasional copperhead.

SOUTH CENTRAL KANSAS

Wichita Walk (29)

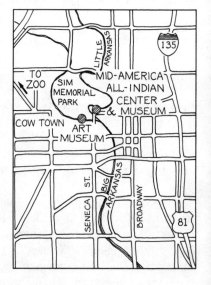

Directions: The walk begins in downtown Wichita at the fork of the Big Arkansas (pronounced in this state "are-KAN-ziss") and Little Arkansas rivers.

Best Season: April and May, and September and October. Summer is also nice, but it can be very hot.

Length: About 3 miles; allow at least half a day so you can visit the museum and restored area of town.

Degree of Difficulty: Easy.

Highlights: A fascinating art museum and a restored nineteenth-century cattle town are among the sites on this walk.

Home to such companies as Cessna, Beech, and Learjet, Wichita is perhaps most famous as a center of aircraft manufacturing. But its history as an Old West cattle town has not been forgotten. From about 1870 to 1880, Wichita was a true town of the Old West, a stop for the cattle and cattlemen of Texas on their way to markets in the east. As part of this walk you will get a firsthand glimpse of what life was like in those colorful days of the wild west in Wichita's historic Cow Town, a restored area of nineteenth-century buildings in the center of downtown.

The walk begins at the 40-foot statue of the *Keeper of the Plains,* at the Mid-America All-Indian Center, 650 N. Seneca. It's interesting to recall as you gaze at this five-ton sculpture of an Indian, his arms stretching toward the sky, that the state motto of Kansas is "To the stars through difficulties." This impressive tribute to native Americans is the work of the late Wichita sculptor Blackbear Bosin. For more information on Wichita's Indian history, visit the Mid-America All-Indian Center where you will find exhibits of nearly all aspects of Indian culture.

Catercorner to the Indian Center is the Wichita Art Museum, a contemporary structure that looks like a collection of triangular black prisms. Many of the works inside are those of contemporary American artists, but there are also permanent displays of the work of western artists Charles M. Russell and Frederic Remington.

Just west of the museum and in marked contrast to its slick, modern exterior is the restored area of Cow Town. Nominator Shirley Condiff explains that there were a number of buildings dating from the 1800s which the city of Wichita wanted to preserve, so they moved them all to one section and restored them. There are now about forty authentically restored buildings, including a newspaper office, a mortuary, a blacksmith shop, a saloon, a doctor's office and, most recently, a grain elevator. "It's a living history museum," Shirley says. "At times you may find cancan dancers or musicians providing entertainment from that period." Thursday through Sunday nights the Empire House Theatre features a melodrama. One of the most recent titles was *Treasures Along the Arkansas* or *This Mine is Mine.* "They are hilarious," Shirley says. "You even get popcorn to throw at the villains."

Across from Cow Town is Sim Memorial Park, which includes a walking fitness trail with twenty exercise stations. East of the park is Botanica, a botanical garden which opened in 1987 and includes several acres of both formal and informal gardens, fountains, and an atrium fountain surrounded by orchids.

Shirley suggests that you fit in a visit to the Sedgwick County Zoo during your stay in Wichita. It's a natural habitat zoo with jungle outback and realistic recreations of scenes from Africa and Asia. "Walkers would love to spend a day at this zoo," Shirley says. "They can even picnic along the lake."

EASTERN KANSAS

University of Kansas Campus Walk (30)

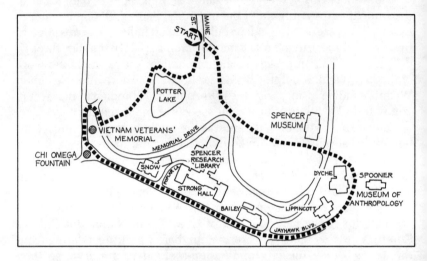

Directions: The University of Kansas is located in the town of Lawrence, midway between Topeka and Kansas City. From I-70 (the Kansas Turnpike), take the West Lawrence exit and go south on Iowa Street to Ninth Street. Turn left (east) and drive 1 mile. Turn right (south) on Main Street and go three blocks. Park in one of the lots near the football stadium.

Best Season: "This is an all-seasons walk," says nominator Wayne Feuerborn, "but it's particularly enjoyable in the spring and fall, or after a fresh snowfall."

Length: 1½ miles; from forty minutes to four hours (if you visit the museums).

Degree of Difficulty: Easy.

Highlights: A relaxing walk in a friendly campus environment.

"This serene campus walk is very relaxing and peaceful," says Wayne Feuerborn, "and the well-maintained grounds form a vast garden."

To begin the walk, take one of the many sidewalks that lead from Memorial Stadium up the hill to the neo-Gothic, limestone-faced Campanile, where you'll enjoy a wonderful view of the Kaw River Valley to the north, as well as glimpses of downtown Lawrence.

"From the Campanile," Wayne says, "take a sidewalk back down the hill heading east through the tree grove. This leads to the Spencer Museum of Art. After visiting the museum, cross Mississippi Street and take the staircase up the hill between Dyche Hall and the Kansas Union. Dyche Hall is the home of the Natural History Museum, one of the most popular tourist attractions in the state of Kansas. Directly across the street is the Museum of Anthropology in Spooner Hall, the oldest building on campus. Spooner Hall is Romanesque in design and is listed in the *National Register of Historic Places*. Both of these museums invite you to stroll through their vast historical collections.

"Return to Jayhawk Boulevard and continue your walk along this tree-lined street, which leads through the heart of the campus. Along this part of the walk, you will see students, staff, and faculty members who are scrambling to class, waiting for the bus, or enjoying the sunshine. This is a very friendly place; many will stop and say hello. One of the most prominent gathering places is the staircase decorated with planters in front of Wescoe Hall, popularly known as 'Wescoe Beach.' Many renovated early-twentieth-century limestone-faced buildings line this route. Between the buildings, you can catch views of the Kaw Valley to the north or the Wakarusa Valley to the south.

"At the terminus of Jayhawk Boulevard is the Chi Omega Fountain. When you reach the fountain, continue your journey to the north along West Campus Road. At the first stop sign, turn right and continue down the road about 100 feet to the Vietnam Veterans' Memorial. From this point, make your own path down the hill to Potter Lake where you can enjoy a moment or two of solitude on the richly landscaped lawn surrounding the lake. From here, it's an easy walk back to your car."

EASTERN KANSAS

Dove Roost Trail (31)

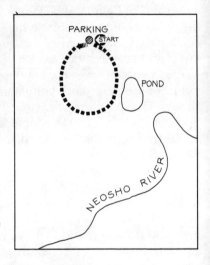

Directions: The trail is located in the Flint Hills National Wildlife Refuge, west of Kansas City and east of Emporia. Take I-35 to exit 144, the Hartford/Neosho River exit. Drive 8 miles south to refuge headquarters in the northwest corner of Hartford. It is well marked.

Best Season: Spring and fall.

Length: The trail is 1 mile, but allow at least a half day to explore this unique and beautiful wildlife refuge.

Degree of Difficulty: Easy.

Highlights: Wildlife and waterfowl abound in this peaceful, scenic protected area.

"There's a lot packed into this easy, 1-mile walk," says David Wiseman, who nominated it. The trail, aptly named for the morning doves which roost in the hedge trees, follows a gravel path through tall prairie grasses which can reach as high as six or seven feet. ("They average about four feet," David says.) The landscape then changes to a deciduous forest of oak, elm, and ash trees.

Then, almost as a surprise, the path leads to a small, five-acre pond where you'll see ducks and geese and maybe spot a deer or two. "In the late fall and early winter (November through January)," David says, "walkers armed with binoculars have a chance to sight bald eagles." In fact, every January, the Kansas Audubon Chapter plans an eagle watching day, complete with hike and lecture. For more information, write the Wildlife Refuge at P.O. Box 128, Hartford, Kansas 66854.

Most of the refuge's 18,500 acres are open to the walker. However, from mid-October to the first week in February, 9,000 acres are designated as a waterfowl sanctuary and are closed to the public. All year, however, there are many wonderful places to view the hundreds of thousands of ducks and geese who visit the refuge on their annual migrations. There's also an artificial lake designed by the U.S. Army Corps of Engineers to serve as a flood-control lake. There is fishing on the Neosho River and camping sites are available. "But camping here is only for the hardy," cautions David. "There are no bathrooms, showers, running water, or jacuzzis!" In addition to poison ivy and ticks, David points out that there are poisonous snakes in the refuge—copperheads, rattlers, and cottonmouths. But no one has been hurt by them.

EASTERN KANSAS

Perry Lake Trail (32)

Directions: The trail is located 18 miles northeast of Topeka in Longview Park near Ozawkie. From Topeka, take Route 24 east to Route 4 north, then to Route 92 east to County Road 1029 south.

Best Season: Fall, winter, spring.

Length: 8 miles one way. Nominator Mobe Rucker says you can leave another car at the end of the trail in a "relay system," or hike the road back (3 miles) to your car.

Degree of Difficulty: Easy.

Highlights: Beautiful woodland walk with scenic views of Perry Lake.

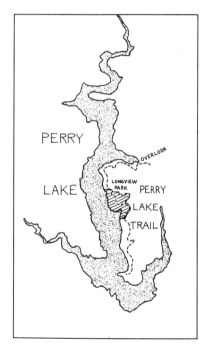

Perry Lake, with its 12,200 surface acres, is the fourth largest lake in Kansas and this relaxing woodland hike takes you to an overlook from which there's a superb view of the lake and the limestone ledges. One of several National Recreation Trails, Perry Lake Trail was originally 14.5 miles long, but a 30-mile loop has been added, making the trail more accessible to more people.

Mobe Rucker, who submitted this walk, likes the 8-mile stretch from Longview Park best because it has such diversity of terrain. The trail starts in a shady wooded area and then winds past coves and across an old field that used to be a hay meadow. From there it leads to other fields which are still mowed for hay and then on into another wooded area and up to the overlook where you have the wonderful view of Perry Lake.

The forested hills of northern red oak, hickory, and walnut are more mature than the woods usually found in Kansas and they make fall a particularly beautiful time of year to hike the trail. Mobe says winter is also a great time because "the woodpeckers are very active and the owls start nesting." In spring, the forest floor is covered with wildflowers, including violets, Dutchman's-breeches, lilies, mayapples, jack-in-the-pulpits, and many more.

The U.S. Army Corps of Engineers maintains campsites at Perry Lake. If you plan to stay overnight, write them at Box 115, Route 1, Perry, Kansas 66073.

Louisiana

SOUTHWESTERN LOUISIANA

Creole Nature Trail's Marsh Nature Trail (33)

Directions: The trail is located in the Sabine Wildlife Refuge. Take I-10 to Highway 27 south in Sulphur, Louisiana.

Best Season: Spring and fall.

Length: 1½ miles. Allow about two hours to really become acquainted with this fascinating marshland.

Degree of Difficulty: Moderate. The marshlands are wild and primitive.

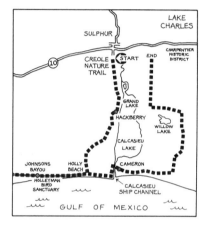

Highlights: An abundance of wildlife. According to nominator Butch Fox Willis, "In the springtime baby alligators pop up around their mothers and are close enough for you to take excellent pictures of them. In the fall, duck and geese come in by the tens of thousands."

Along this unique trail the walker has an opportunity to see the largest collection of wildlife and marsh flowers in a natural marshlands setting found anywhere in the country. A paved walkway leads right into the marshes, over bridges, and onto observation decks. Alligators may block the trail from time to time, but they've never been known to hurt anyone. It's best to keep your distance, however. They may look clumsy or lazy or slow, but alligators can move amazingly fast when they want to, and they can be dangerous. Don't approach them or touch them. To gauge their length, estimate the number of inches from the tip of the snout to the line across the base of their eyes: One inch equals one foot in length.

As you follow the coastline of the Gulf of Mexico along the Creole

Nature Trail, you will see evidence such as tracks or droppings of other animals as well. Raccoon, nutria, rabbit, muskrat, and even mink all live and play nearby. You may even catch a glimpse of these animals themselves, although they are more likely to be about at night.

Midway along the trail, you'll come to the town of Cameron, where you'll see shrimp boats and can visit a shrimp processing plant. A ferry will take you across the Calcasieu Ship Channel, a narrow inlet of the Gulf of Mexico, where, if you're lucky, you'll get a chance to see porpoise frolicking.

The trail continues on to Holly Beach, known as the "Cajun Riviera." Here you can stroll along the water's edge, sunbathe, swim, collect shells, or fish to your heart's content. West of Holly Beach is Johnsons Bayou and the Holleyman Bird Sanctuary. Nestled in the shelter of an old beach ridge called a "chenier," the sanctuary is a feeding grounds for millions of songbirds. The *chenier* ("a place where oaks grow") gets its name from the moss-draped oaks which somehow manage to survive the salty atmosphere of the Gulf.

After your walk through the marsh, stop in Hackberry, the self-proclaimed "Crab Capital of the World," and if there's time, visit Sulphur, home of the Brimestone Museum, which features the "Frash process" for mining sulphur. Lake Charles, just east of Sulphur off I-10, is also worth a visit. Here you can enjoy some of the best Cajun cuisine in Louisiana, stroll through the historic Charpentier district, a twenty-square-block area of Victorian charm in the Lake Charles style, or, if you come in the spring, participate in a trip to the past during "Contraband Days." For the first two weeks of May, Lake Charles is transformed into a party, celebrating the days of the "Gentleman Pirate," Jean Lafitte. Parades, boat races, a jazz fest, and arts and crafts shows are just a part of the fun.

SOUTHEASTERN LOUISIANA

Downtown Baton Rouge (34)

Directions: The walk begins at the War Memorial of the *USS Kidd*, a naval war destroyer used in both World War II and the Korean war. This is Catfish Town, part of Old Baton Rouge on the Mississippi Riverfront.

Best Season: Year-round.

Length: About 1 mile, but allow time to browse.

Degree of Difficulty: Easy.

Highlights: Two capitols in Louisiana's capital.

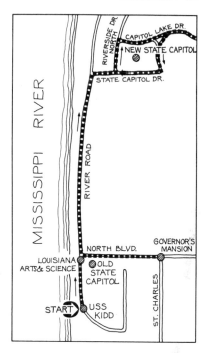

Founded in 1719, Baton Rouge was alternately French, English, and Spanish until it was acquired by the United States in the 1800s. It became Louisiana's state capital in 1849. Today it is a lovely city—bustling with activity and bursting with the warmth and color that come from an abundance of sweetly scented blossoms—a far cry from the Indian village that French explorer Pierre Lemoyne, *sieur d'Iberville*, saw when he arrived in 1699. Apparently the Indians used to hang their game from a small cypress tree in the center of the village, and some believe that one of Lemoyne's men saw this skinny tree—stained with the blood of animals—and called the place *baton rouge,* or "red stick." But another story has it that the name came from a large cypress tree whose bark had been removed so that it stood like a large "red stick" above the Mississippi River.

Beauregard Town was to have been the center of Baton Rouge, and a town square was to have been built here. But Union soldiers occupied Baton Rouge during the Civil War, and for a brief period Opelousas became the capital and then Shreveport. It was not until after the Civil War that Baton Rouge once again became the state capital, and by that time plans for the town square in Beauregard Town had been discarded.

From the War Memorial of the *USS Kidd*, nominator Kathy Hogan suggests you pay a visit to the Arts and Science Center, a riverside museum and former railroad station which houses art exhibits, an Egyptian mummy, and elegant old train compartments.

Across the street at the corner of River Road and North Boulevard is the Old State Capitol. Now under renovation, the original building was constructed in 1849. It was destroyed by fire and rebuilt in 1882. Outside are beautiful gardens and a view of the Mississippi River.

From the Old State Capitol, walk up North Boulevard to St. Charles Street where you'll find the former Governor's Mansion. Built by Huey (the "Kingfish") Long in 1930, it is furnished with Louisiana antiques, and each room is dedicated to a different Louisiana governor, none more colorful or controversial than Long himself.

About a mile from the riverfront on State Capitol Drive is the New State Capitol, where Long was assassinated in 1935 by Dr. Carl A. Weiss. Built in 1932, the New State Capitol rises 450 feet (34 stories) above the Mississippi River Valley, making it the tallest state capitol in the country. Steps leading up to the front entrance commemorate each of the fifty states, and an observation deck on the twenty-seventh floor overlooks the Memorial Gardens, 27 acres of formal gardens on the capitol grounds. "This is a great place for a family to walk and enjoy the azaleas and oaks on a Sunday afternoon," Kathy says. "There's a long hill in front of a statue of Huey Long that kids love to roll down. Capitol Lake, just behind the capitol, is a peaceful place to relax and watch the ducks."

Inside the capitol, you'll find a Visitor Information Center where you can get all the information you need about your visit to Baton Rouge and the surrounding area.

Kathy loves to walk around Baton Rouge because "the people are very friendly and the landscaping is beautiful. People here are very conscious of how things look, and the azaleas and oak trees draped with hanging moss are important to everyone. And," she adds, "there's a lot of spirit in Baton Rouge. It's a big sports town with LSU football, basketball, and baseball. We have a saying here: It never rains in Tiger Stadium on a Saturday night!"

A mile and a half south of downtown Baton Rouge is Louisiana State University, where you can meet Mike the Tiger, the LSU mascot in his elaborate "cage" which features a stream, trees, and even a cave. LSU students raised hundreds of thousands of dollars in order to give Mike this luxurious home.

SOUTHEASTERN LOUISIANA

New Orleans:
A New Look at the Old Quarter (35)

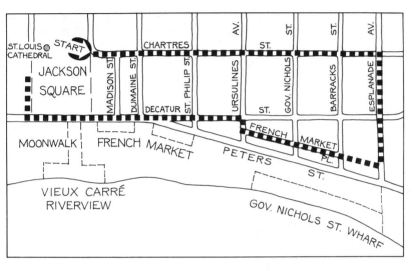

Directions: The walk begins at St. Louis Cathedral on Chartres Street in Jackson Square.

Best Season: Year-round.

Length: Fifteen or so city blocks; allow at least a half day to take in the delights of the French Quarter.

Degree of Difficulty: Easy.

Highlights: A never-ending stimulus to the senses awaits the walker around every corner.

This walk, nominated by J. Michael Kenny, begins at St. Louis Cathedral, whose spire is the tallest point in the French Quarter, or Vieux Carré, and will act as a beacon to keep you oriented during the walk. In front of the church is the Place d'Armes, or Jackson Square, which is bordered by a wrought-iron fence covered by an ever-changing display of paintings and works-in-progress by local artists.

Walk diagonally across the square to the Lower Pontalba Apartment Building, one of a pair of identical three-story buildings which were built in the eighteenth century by the Baroness Pontalba and which later became the first apartment buildings in the United States. On the ground level are numerous galleries, shops, and eateries. One of these is La Madeleine, a brick-oven bakery that J. Michael says "is not to be missed." Next to La Madeleine is Brocato's, a family-run Italian ice cream and cookie business that dates from 1905.

Walk back down Chartres Street, past a used-record store, punk-hair salons, more art galleries, and various other shops. Be sure to glance in between the buildings to catch a glimpse of the courtyards, fountains, and balconies that were a hallmark of early Spanish architecture. At the corner of Chartres Street and Ursulines Avenue is the Convent of the Ursulines Monastery, home to an order of nuns who first came from France in the 1700s. Across the street is the Beauregard-Keyes House, which was built in 1826 by General G. T. Beauregard of the Confederate Army and was later owned by Frances Parkinson Keyes, who immortalized New Orleans in her novels and, more specifically, the restaurant of Antoine Alciatoire in the book *Dinner at Antoine's*. The restaurant, located on St. Louis Street, is still being run by Antoine's descendants.

Continue down Chartres Street to Governor Nichols Street, and walk right one block to Decatur. Turn left and walk to the old U.S. Mint between Barracks Street and Esplanade Avenue, where coins for the Confederacy were once minted; now the building houses the Archives and various offices. J. Michael says that the "Streetcar Named Desire" is on permanent display there.

Near the old Mint, every Friday, Saturday, and Sunday, is the French Market Flea Market, where you can browse to your heart's content and buy just about anything from original paintings to "antique" comic books. Housed in one of the sheds that was once part of the original French Market, this is still the place where restaurant buyers and chefs come for the freshest produce—eggplant, creole tomatoes, garlic, okra. Everything they need is found here in abundance.

Leaving the market, you are suddenly filled with the sights and sounds of old New Orleans. J. Michael describes them for us: "pastel-fronted shops and buildings; delicately ornate ironwork on balconies;

red-tiled roofs; the sounds of ships' horns passing on the Mississippi just a few yards away; jazz wafting through the air from nearby clubs, bars, and patios; the smell of coffee roasting and bread baking, mixed with the scent of flowers and the aroma of oils and spices."

Walk back now on Decatur where you'll be greeted by an offering of thick, sweet pecan praline or the olive-onion-caper sandwich, with salami, Swiss, and ham, called a *muffellata*. Last but certainly not least is the famous Café du Monde, home of the unforgettably delicious, powdered *beignet* and "high-octane" café au lait. Across the street from Café du Monde is your beacon and home point, the towering spire of St. Louis Cathedral.

SOUTHEASTERN LOUISIANA

New Orleans:
Bayou St. John Waterway Walk (36)

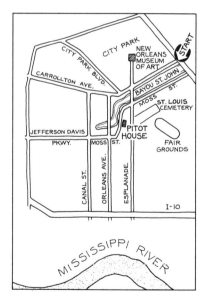

Directions: You can get to the Bayou St. John from the French Market in the Old Quarter by walking east on Decatur Street to Esplanade Avenue. Esplanade begins at the Mississippi River and ends about 2 miles later at City Park. This walk follows the Bayou St. John, which makes a graceful curve from the left of Esplanade Avenue (as you face the park entrance).

Best Season: Year-round. Try any morning, weekend, or late afternoon.

Length: From ¾ mile to 3 miles; one to four hours.

Degree of Difficulty: Easy.

Highlights: The walk features historic architecture amid a peaceful bayou setting rich with the scent of magnolia, sweet olive, and other intoxicating flowering trees and shrubs.

Nominator J. Michael Kenny particularly likes this walk early in the morning on a foggy fall day, but he recommends it anytime of year as a delightful way to relax and slow down the quick pace that often characterizes a visit to the tempting city of New Orleans.

The walk begins at the entrance to the 1,500-acre City Park, which is actually a former plantation bequeathed to New Orleans in 1850. An equestrian statue of General G. T. Beauregard, C.S.A., stands at the entryway. Inside the park you'll find the New Orleans Museum of Art, one of the last wooden carousel rides in America, four golf courses, reflective pools with bronze statuary, the Rose Garden, and meandering lagoons dotted with two-wheeler paddleboats, parading swans, ducks and geese, and people fishing along the banks. But before you lose yourself in the delights of City Park, let's take the bayou walk.

Begin to the left of the park's entrance and follow the bayou as it curves gently through the Faubourg St. John, a residential area that was first laid out in 1809. Stately old homes can be seen along the levees, and the heavy floral fragrances from the many flowering trees and shrubs will make you feel as elegant and beautiful as the old mansions themselves. Plaques are unobtrusively displayed along the walk to show you the dates of some of these wonderful old homes. At one of the S curves in the Bayou near the old, once-rotating steel bridge (for pedestrian traffic only), there's a commemorative plaque indicating that this was once a portage used by Indians who came from the lakes north of New Orleans to the Mississippi River for trapping, trade, and commerce. The Indians showed it to Sieurs de Bienville and Iberville in 1699.

One of the most interesting homes on the walk is the Pitot House which dates from 1799 and is one of the few West Indies–style homes on the bayou. James Pitot, who became the first mayor of the newly incorporated city of New Orleans, bought the house in 1810. Today the Pitot House is an exquisitely restored plantation home, furnished in a style typical of New Orleans in the 1830s. It is open to the public Wednesday through Saturday, 10 a.m. to 3 p.m.

A few doors down from Pitot House is the Evariste Blanc House which was built around 1824. A good example of the Classical Revival Plantation style, this house is used today as the rectory of Our Lady of the Most Holy Rosary.

J. Michael suggests you walk a few steps down Moss Street (which borders Bayou St. John) to the corner of Grand Route St. John. At 300 Moss Street stands the Old Spanish Customs House which was given to New Orleans in 1709 (ten years prior to the founding of the city). It served as a plantation house from 1736 to 1807 when it was renovated by an architect who had remodeled the (Spanish) Customs House in downtown New Orleans. It is believed he used some of the boards from that house, thus the name Old Spanish Customs House, despite the building's West Indian style.

When you've finished your walk along the bayou, J. Michael reminds you to explore the wonderful City Park.

NORTHERN LOUISIANA

Shreveport: Clyde Fant Walking and Jogging Trail (37)

Directions: The trail is located in downtown Shreveport and begins at the Convention Complex.

Best Season: Year-round.

Length: About 7 miles one way.

Degree of Difficulty: Easy.

Highlights: This scenic walk along the Red River includes an exercise parcourse and picnic areas.

For a change of pace during your visit to Shreveport, nominator Evelyn Howard suggests you walk on the Clyde Fant Walking and Jogging Trail. Designated a National Scenic Trail, this 7-mile route can be broken up by taking any number of the loops or double-backs available. It's a great way to get some exercise and enjoy Shreveport from a unique perspective. At the start of the walk, you may want to explore the R. S. Barnwell Garden and Art Center, a combination art and gar-

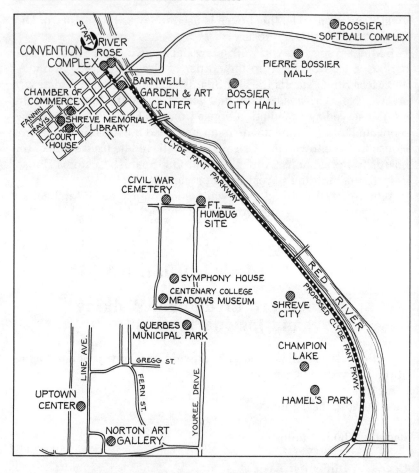

den area which houses exquisite permanent plant displays as well as seasonal exhibits. You can also take a ride on the *River Rose*, an old-fashioned paddlewheeler which cruises up and down the Red River daily.

It was a riverboat captain named Henry Miller Shreve who was, in effect, responsible for Shreveport's existence. In 1833, the government hired Shreve to break a 165-mile log jam which blocked the Red River and which had been christened the "Great Raft." Shreve and his men were successful by means of a "snag boat" that Shreve himself had invented. Two years later the Caddo Indians gave 640 acres of land in the area to a man called Larkin Edwards, who acted as their interpreter, and, subsequently, Edwards sold the land to eight men, one of whom was Henry Shreve. Shreve's land was incorporated into Shreve Town Company and was renamed Shreveport in 1837.

Before leaving Shreveport, don't miss the American Rose Center located just west of the city on Jefferson Paige Road. This 118 acre garden is the largest rose garden in the country, and it is here that the American Rose Garden Society evaluates new hybrids and registers new varieties of the nation's official flower, the rose. Pathways through the woods open up to thirty-five different gardens, each unique in design, with gazebos and benches where you can sit down and enjoy the flowers, which are in bloom from April through December.

NORTHERN LOUISIANA

Poverty Point (38)

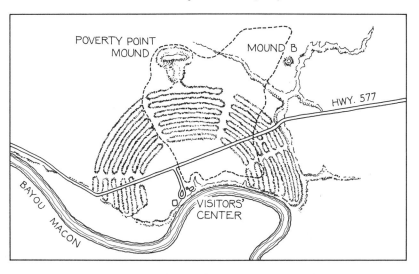

Directions: Take I-20 to Delhi, and head north on Highway 17 to Epps. Turn right at the light, then left at the bridge (Hwy. 577) and follow signs to Poverty Point. The trail begins at the visitors' center (which also serves as the laboratory where Indian artifacts are studied).

Best Season: Year-round.

Length: Just over 2 miles.

Degree of Difficulty: Easy.

Highlights: Mounds and artifacts left by Indians some 3,000 years ago make this the oldest and largest prehistoric site in North America.

Poverty Point is a 400-acre plantation dating from the 1800s, which was owned by the Guier family. Its name is not unusual, nominator Mary Borden tells us. Apparently a number of plantations had names like Poverty Point or Hard Times Plantation or Hard Luck Plantation; the names were probably used by owners to reflect the difficulties encountered when growing cotton.

But even more interesting than the chance to glimpse plantation life in the 1800s are the earthen mounds and rows of ridges at Poverty Point. There are six concentric ridges which range from about five to ten feet high and are some three-quarters of a mile wide. They were made by carrying soil in large cane baskets and depositing them in a specific place. It is thought that these ridges were used by Indians about 3,000 years ago, perhaps for ceremonial purposes. Some archaeologists believe people actually lived on the ridges, but no one knows why. Halfway through the walk, you'll reach a ceremonial earthen mound, shaped like a bird.

The walking trail will also take you by Sarah's Hill, a cemetery dating back to the 1800s and named for Sarah Wilson Guier, who is buried there.

Before you begin your walk, visit the laboratory and visitors' center where the walk begins. There the artifacts from this prehistoric site are studied and analyzed. It has been learned, for example, that the Indians made clay balls, dried them in the sun, and then placed them in fire to heat them. Once they were hot enough, the balls were put in a pit and food was cooked on top of them. You can watch a film about the area and see thousands of artifacts in the museum.

If you have time after your visit to Poverty Point, get back on I-20 and head west to Monroe where you can visit the Louisiana Purchase Gardens and Zoo. Here you can walk through formal gardens and wander along pathways that lead through oak groves. The zoo is an excellent place not only to see rare animals but also to get an interesting history lesson because it describes events leading up to the Louisiana Purchase in 1803.

WEST CENTRAL LOUISIANA

Hodges Gardens Walking Trails (39)

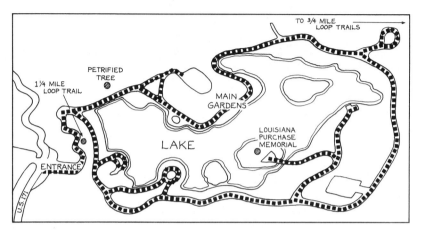

Directions: The gardens are located 12 miles south of Many and 18 miles north of Leesville on Highway 171.

Best Season: Year-round.

Length: There are three marked hiking trails in the gardens: a 1¼-mile loop and two ¾-mile loops. In addition there are gravel pathways throughout the gardens and 10 miles of roadway.

Degree of Difficulty: Easy.

Highlights: Flowering gardens, forests, and creeks provide a peaceful setting (and there is also a herd of buffalo to see).

The 4,700-acre Hodges Gardens Botanical Garden and Arboretum was first created by conservationist Andrew Jackson Hodges in the 1940s. Today pebbled walkways wind through the acres of gardens, which are spectacular in every season. In the spring, tulips, azaleas, and dogwoods are in bloom; in the summer, impatiens, begonias, lilies, and roses; in the fall, you'll be greeted by the rich colors of chrysanthemums, as well as bright-red berries on the shrubs; in the winter, you'll see the camelias, pansies, ornamental kale, and cabbage.

The three hiking trails were blazed by Mothers Against Drugs (MAD)—not to be confused with Mothers Against Drunk Driving (MADD)—as part of MAD's Get High on Life Program. The 1¼-mile loop trail begins about 400 yards from the main gate and goes over creek bottoms and fire service roads and through a pine forest. The first ¾-mile-loop trail passes by the picnic area beside buffalo pens where you can see a herd of about thirty to forty buffalo. This trail also goes through the pines and connects to the second ¾-mile loop.

At the entrance to the main garden, there is a petrified tree thought to be thousands of years old. In addition, you'll find a 225-acre lake on the property where fishing boats are available for rental year-round.

The creeks and peaceful waterfalls blend with the spectacular garden displays to make Hodges Gardens a wonderful place to walk. Stacy Brown, who nominated it, says spring is the most popular because the azaleas are out, and there is a marked path leading through the Native Azalea Overlook. But Stacy likes to walk in the gardens all year. "The trails are beautiful," she says. "It's a wonderful place to be by yourself."

For an interesting change of pace, visit Louisiana's oldest city, Natchitoches, which is only about 33 miles from Hodges Gardens. Head back to Many on Route 171 and take Route 6 east to Natchitoches. Located on Cane River Lake, the city was founded in 1714 by Louis Juchereau de St. Denis. It was originally a French military and trading post, and the French influence can still be seen in a walking tour of the historic district, which is charming with its eighteenth- and early nineteenth-century homes sporting the intricate wrought-iron balconies typical of New Orleans. Rogue House, constructed of clay and mud, interspersed with animal hair and Spanish moss packed between cypress beams, is now a museum. Located on the picturesque River Bank Drive, it's worth a visit.

Michigan

UPPER PENINSULA

North Country Trail (40)

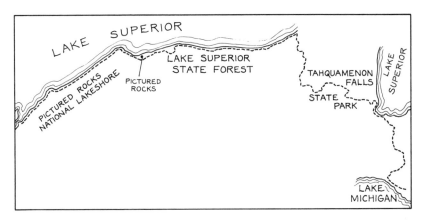

Directions: The eastern Trailhead is 4 miles north of St. Ignace on Forest Route 3104. This walk covers the North Country Trail from the Rivermouth Campground through Tahquamenon Falls State Park, north to Lake Superior and through Pictured Rocks National Lakeshore. A hike such as this requires advance planning. For more information, write: Tahquamenon Falls State Park, S.R. 48, Box 225, Paradise, MI 49768; and Pictured Rocks National Lakeshore, P.O. Box 40, Sand Point, Munsing, MI 49862-0040.

Best Season: Late summer ("There are no bugs, and the rivers are not too risky," says nominator Donald Weiss).

Length: 200 miles, about fourteen days, but the walk can be terminated at various points. For the usual walker (i.e., those of us who don't want to wander too far from civilization), there's a fun-filled 4.5-mile Bridge Walk which begins at St. Ignace every Labor Day.

Degree of Difficulty: The Bridge Walk is easy. Hiking the North Country Trail is difficult: The terrain is sometimes boggy, three rivers must be forded, and the hiker must carry provisions for seven days.

77

Highlights: The North Country Trail is an unparalleled learning experience that stretches the mind and body, gives you a chance to meet wonderful people and affords the incredible satisfaction that comes at the end when you can say, "I did it!"

This trek is definitely not for everyone. Nominator Donald Weiss, who walked it—solo—in 1982, has compiled a list of seven requirements needed to complete the hike successfully: good health, top mental and physical condition, understanding family, ironclad desire to succeed, advance planning, good equipment, and good luck.

Donald began his walk in St. Ignace on Labor Day. Here, on this particular day, there is a walk for everyone. It's the annual 4.5-mile Bridge Walk from St. Ignace to Mackinaw City across the Straits of Mackinac on the Mackinac Bridge. Each year more than 50,000 walkers flood the area for this event. Afterward, be sure to take the ferry from either St. Ignace or Mackinaw City to Mackinac Island, a wonderful place to take a walk through history or just browse in the many shops. For more information about the Bridge Walk, write: Mackinac Bridge Authority, St. Ignace, MI 49781.

Before starting out on the North Country Trail, Donald suggests you prepare yourself for "bear country." He carried a small bell on the bottom of his pack frame to ensure that he would not surprise a she-bear and her cubs along the route. As it turned out, he never saw a bear at all. "They know you're there," a woman who gave him water said, "and they stay away."

Following the blue blazes that mark the trail and guide the walker through a labyrinthine wilderness, Donald was often struck by his dependency on those who had put the blazes in place. Without them, he would have been hopelessly lost. And by the fifth day, he was more than grateful for all the training he had put in prior to the hike. After climbing over extremely rugged terrain and crossing rivers (sometimes twice, first with boots and camera and then back again for backpack, because everything had to be held overhead), he knew that had he not trained, he'd be "thumbing a ride back to St. Ignace." Without a strong back and good legs, it's best to travel by car. Of course, as Donald points out, the motorist can never experience what the trail walker does.

By the ninth day, Donald had reached the shores of Lake Superior and could enjoy a nice easy walk along the beach. The next day he visited the quaint fishing town of Grand Marais where he supped on whitefish, a delicious change from his usual "trail" food. Here he met a bear hunter who was very friendly, as were all the people Donald met on his journey. It's one of the reasons he likes to hike alone. "I'm certain," he says, "I could not have met the people I did if I had had a companion. There seems to be something irresistible about a lone traveler who carries all his needs on his back and whose only means of getting from point A to point B are his own two feet."

At this point, the Grand Sable Dunes area, Donald had trouble following the trail because there are no blazes on the trees in Pictured Rocks National Lakeshore. But the scenery here is fantastic, with the dunes rising as high as 375 feet above the shores of Lake Superior. And the next night a beautiful sunset behind Grand Island provided a fitting reward to the weary traveler. It set the whole western sky ablaze, Donald remembers. "Unfortunately, I cannot photograph all these gorgeous displays of Mother Nature's," he says, "but my friend Bob Moyer of Traverse City put it most aptly when he said, 'The best pictures are the pictures in your mind.' How true. And they will never fade for the 'film is firmly etched.'"

Those interested in hiking the North Country Trail may want to contact Donald directly for more information. Send a stamped, self-addressed envelope to: Donald Weiss, 1512 Mulloy Drive, Addison, IL 60101.

UPPER PENINSULA

Tahquamenon Falls Walkway (41)

Directions: Take I-75 to M-123 to the town of Paradise. Follow signs to the Tahquamenon Falls State Park (about 7 miles from Paradise.)

Best Season: The last two weeks in September.

Length: 1½ miles for the walk to the falls, but there are many longer trails if you want to explore the area in more depth.

Degree of Difficulty: Moderate.

Highlights: The spectacular Tahquamenon Waterfalls, which are nearly 200 feet across and 50 feet high.

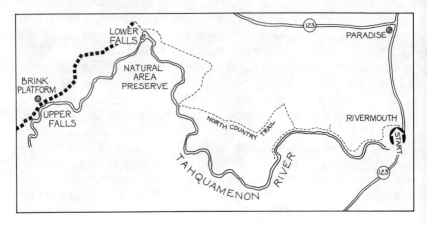

The Tahquamenon "marsh of blueberries" River has played an important part in Michigan's history since the Chippewa Indians first camped along its shores and fished its waters. In the 1800s, lumberjacks floated thousands of logs along the river to lumber mills; these men and their families were the first white settlers in the area. And Henry Wadsworth Longfellow wrote about the river in "The Song of Hiawatha." It was "by the rushing Tahquamenaw" that Hiawatha built his canoe, and it was Hiawatha's friend Kwasind ("the strong one") who cleared the river of debris. Today the Tahquamenon flows through the center of the Tahquamenon Falls State Park and is enjoyed by visitors from all over for its peaceful scenic beauty.

This walk will take you along a paved walkway to the spectacular Upper Falls where steps lead down to the Brink Platform and Waterfall Gorge. These falls are among the largest east of the Mississippi; 5,000 gallons of "golden" water (lit by the sun) per second have been recorded cascading over them.

In autumn, the falls are especially beautiful, the water sparkling under the bright sunlight and reflecting the vivid colors of the foliage on the surrounding trees. Bring your camera; the Brink Platform is a wonderful vantage point for taking photographs.

Four miles downstream from the Upper Falls are the Lower Falls, which are also beautiful. You can rent a rowboat or canoe and paddle out to an island to see the Lower Falls. There is also fishing and camping in the area and there is cross-country skiing in the winter. For more information, write to the Manager, Tahquamenon Falls State Park, Paradise, MI 49768, or call (906) 492-3415.

UPPER PENINSULA

Isle Royale: Island Mine Trail (42)

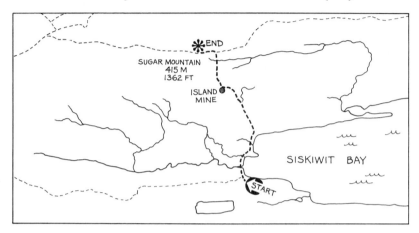

Directions: The trail is located in Isle Royale National Park, some 73 miles north of Houghton in Michigan's Upper Peninsula. Boat service is available from mid-June through Labor Day from Houghton and from Copper Harbor, Michigan, and from Grand Portage, Minnesota, from mid-May through mid-October.

Best Season: July, August, September.

Length: This walk is 5 miles, but there are many walking trails on Isle Royale ranging in length from less than a mile to 40 miles. You can also hike the 70 to 75 miles around the island. Plan to spend at least one day on Isle Royale; it's an experience.

Degree of Difficulty: Moderate to moderately difficult. The terrain can be rocky.

Highlights: Isle Royale is a unique wilderness archipelago. You will see and experience things here you cannot find anywhere else in the country.

Isle Royale is an island of extraordinary wilderness beauty. There are no roads, but more than 170 miles of hiking trails lead into an area of wild animals, virgin forests, and lakes. Wolves and moose are among the animals that roam the island, and their story is an interesting and educational one.

At the turn of the century there were no wolves or moose on Isle Royale. It is thought that the moose arrived in the early 1900s, probably swimming to the island from Canada's mainland. With no predators, the moose proliferated until by the 1930s they had just about destroyed the browse (shoots, twigs, and leaves of shrubs) that sustained them. In 1936, a fire burned the remaining browse, and it looked as though the moose were doomed. But in a twist of "natural" fate, the fire spurred new growth and the browse returned, giving the moose a new lease on life. The animals thrived until, once again, they depleted their food supply. This time they were saved by wolves who crossed over to the island via an ice bridge that was formed during the unusually cold winter of 1948–1949. The wolves, who kill those moose which are old or sick or weak, help preserve the health of the rest of the population. This is just one example of the highly complex and unique system of nature that exists on Isle Royale.

People, too, have played a role in the ecological development of the island. Indians used to mine copper here by hammering at it with hand-held cobbles. Later "modern" copper mining replaced the Indians' more primitive but less harmful methods. During the era of modern mining, large areas of the island were burned and white settlements were developed. Commercial fishing became important in the 1830s, and in the early twentieth century the island became a popular summer resort. Finally, in 1940, Isle Royale became a national park. Today our role is to observe and learn, not to touch.

The 5-mile Island Mine Trail, which heads north from the Siskiwit Bay Campground and crosses the Big Siskiwit River, is one that many people particularly like. It passes by Senter Point, where you can see the remains of the old powder house where explosives were stored when Island Mine was in operation. The mine itself is about 2 miles from the shore. Be careful as you explore this area because vegetation has grown over some of the open mine shafts, making them difficult to spot. From Carnelian Beach the trail climbs to Sugar Mountain; near the end is a beautiful forest of sugar maples and yellow birch.

NORTHERN MICHIGAN

Grand Traverse Bay Walk (43)

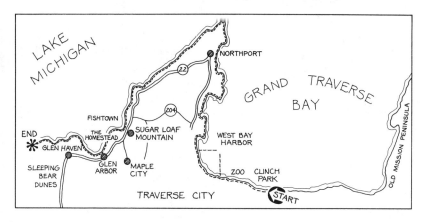

Directions: Take U.S. 31 to Traverse City, where the walk begins.

Best Season: Spring through fall.

Length: Varies. You can walk the southern end of the bay or jog on up the peninsula. It's easy to spend a whole day in the area.

Degree of Difficulty: Easy.

Highlights: "A brisk walk along the water at sunrise is a great way to start the day," says nominator J. P. Martin.

Paved walkways have been built for this walk along the water, which was nominated by J. P. Martin, but she and her daughter, Jamie, prefer to walk barefoot on the "sugar-sand" beach where they stop to watch for a variety of native waterfowl or just to spend time together skipping stones. There is access to the beach from Clinch Park on the southern shore of Grand Traverse Bay. You'll find a zoo there, too, featuring animals and waterfowl native to Michigan, and a museum of Indian and pioneer artifacts.

Traverse City, known as the "Cherry Capital of the World," is surrounded by more than 500,000 cherry trees which are, of course, spectacular in April and May when they are in blossom.

J. P. Martin calls northwest Michigan a "veritable walker's paradise, with something for every age and level of walking experience." The walk along the southern end of Grand Traverse Bay is for everyone. For the walker looking for more of a challenge, J. P. suggests a visit to Sleeping Bear Dunes National Park in Glen Arbor, just a half-hour drive from Traverse City. "The golden sand dunes," she says, "start just a few steps from the parking area and reach to the skies, offering a fun-filled 'workout.'" She recommends bringing a bathing suit, because once you're at the top, Lake Michigan is just a "stone's throw" away. The Sleeping Bear Dunes are open daily from May through September. J. P. likes to be there in the early evening when the tourists have "dissipated and the sand is deliciously cool on your feet."

For the runner, J. P. suggests a jog on the Old Mission Peninsula, which winds along Grand Traverse Bay through miles of luxurious summer homes as well as homes of year-round residents ("Some of these people have even set out benches to accommodate the weary runner," says J. P.), and then into the vast cherry orchards. The road is flat for the most part and offers an almost continuous view of the beautiful bay. Throughout the spring, there are various foot races on the peninsula and one marathon.

NORTHERN MICHIGAN

Hartwick Pines (44)

Directions: Take I-75 to the Hartwick Pines Interchange, just north of the town of Grayling. Turn right on Hartwick Pines Road (M-93) which leads to the park.

Best Season: Summer and fall.

Length: About 1½ miles; allow an hour or two.

Degree of Difficulty: Easy.

Highlights: The Mighty Monarch, a 300-year-old white pine tree, is the central feature on this walk through Michigan's only remaining virgin pine forest.

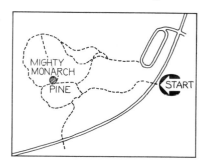

This walk, nominated by Chuck Budd, takes you into a forest of white pine, the only remaining stand of such virgin growth left in Michigan. Here you'll see the giant Mighty Monarch, a 300-year-old pine that stands 155 feet tall. You'll also be able to visit logging camp exhibits which recreate camping life and feature logging equipment, the quarters of the camp boss, a bunkhouse, blacksmith shop, and saw filer's workshop.

The significance of all this can best be appreciated by an awareness of history. As the eastern forests were depleted, Michigan's abundant white pine became more and more in demand, and by 1869, Michigan was producing more lumber than any other state. The effect of this, of course, was to boost Michigan's economy, stimulating the development of a complex transportation system and spurring the growth of many cities and towns. A more vivid picture of the impact this lumber boom had on the state's economy can be seen by comparing it to California's Gold Rush: The dollar value of Michigan's timber was greater than all the gold mined in California during the same period.

While this may have been good for people (although the life of a logger was far from easy), it was disastrous for the trees. Only 85 acres of what was once a vast landscape of Norway and white pine escaped the axe, and these acres were further reduced by age and storms. Today just 49 acres remain, preserved as a reminder of the influence people can have, especially if they act without foresight or in ignorance. This information is food for thought as you walk through the beautiful Hartwick pine forest.

Hartwick Pines State Park, with 9,800 acres, is the largest in Michigan's Lower Peninsula. In addition to its historical significance, the park is a wonderful place to walk; its high rolling hills provide a perfect vantage point from which to observe the scenic Au Sable River Valley. For more information on the various trails through the park, write to the Park Manager, Hartwick Pines State Park, Route 3, Box 3840, Grayling, MI 49738, or call (517) 348-7068.

SOUTHEASTERN MICHIGAN

Hidden Lake Gardens Walk (45)

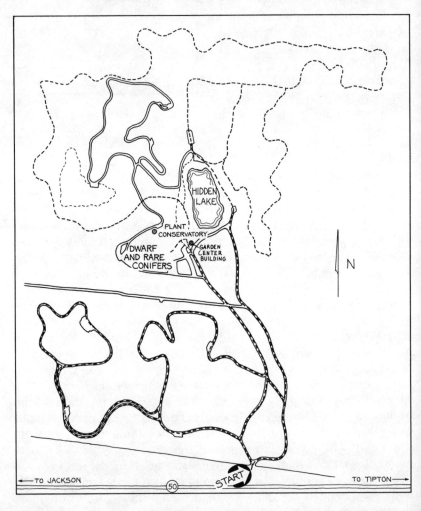

Directions: Located in Tipton, Michigan, Hidden Lake Gardens belongs to Michigan State University. Take U.S. 23 to U.S. 223 to Adrian. Head north on Route 52 at Adrian, then west on Route 50 to the west side of Tipton. Watch for signs to the gardens.

Best Season: Spring and summer.

Length: 7 miles; allow about three hours.

Degree of Difficulty: Easy.

Highlights: Paved rolling driveways lead through orchards and acres of gorgeous flowering plants and trees.

Hidden Lake Gardens are located in what are known as the Irish Hills of Southeastern Michigan. The gardens originated in 1926 when the late Harry A. Fee, a prominent businessman from Adrian, bought the property and personally began supervising the planting and landscaping of its gardens. Fee's purpose was to create a unique area of great beauty. In 1945, Mr. and Mrs. Fee donated the gardens to Michigan State University, which has maintained their beauty and preserved them for the study of horticulture and landscaping. Each year the collection of plants and trees is expanded, and the original 226 acres now totals over 670.

As you walk through the trails that wind throughout the gardens, you'll see a wide variety of plants that include crabapples, cherry trees, hawthorne, junipers, lilacs, maples, azaleas, and roses. There is also a unique collection of dwarf and rare conifers, magnolia trees, spruce, willows, pines, and rhododendrons. As you can imagine, this wonderful variety and the beauty of the lake itself (almost hidden behind the shrubs and trees) makes Hidden Lake Gardens an inspirational setting.

There is also a Plant Conservatory with some 8,000 feet of glass, a display lobby and two domes, a 50-foot-high tropical dome and a 30-foot-high arid dome, each displaying an array of plants appropriate to the different climates. There's an information center at the Hidden Lakes Garden Center Building, as well as a reference library, an auditorium, meeting rooms, and an exhibit concourse. Nearby are demonstration areas where a variety of bulbs, annuals, and perennials for home gardening are planted. If you are planning a home garden, this would be a great place to ask for ideas and advice.

CENTRAL MICHIGAN

Dow Gardens Walk (46)

Directions: Take I-75 to U.S. 10 to the city of Midland. The entrance to the gardens is at the corner of Eastman and St. Andrews roads in Midland.

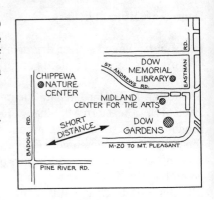

Best Season: Spring and summer.

Length: 1 mile; about 1 hour.

Degree of Difficulty: Easy.

Highlights: Formal flower gardens ablaze with color.

The Dow Gardens originated in 1899 when Dr. Herbert H. Dow, founder of the Dow Chemical Company, planted the first tree. He intended to create an ever-changing garden area, and today that is just what Dow Gardens are—an ever-changing array of beauty. The 66 acres are constantly being renewed, and new plants are continually being introduced. The gardens are open from 10 a.m. to sunset seven days a week, and visitors are encouraged to walk *everywhere* and to explore the entire area, which is designed to show the relationship of human beings to nature. To this end, there are numerous horticultural programs for both children and adults. Some will help you plan your own home garden, whether it be a garden of vegetables or herbs or a small greenhouse for flowering plants. The gardens also provide an internship program where future gardeners, horticulturists, landscape architects, and students of urban forestry and landscape horticulture can gain firsthand knowledge and experience.

Alongside the gardens is the Midland Center for the Arts, which includes a 386-seat theater and a four-level Hall of Ideas, which is an art, history, and science museum. Also near the gardens is the Dow Memorial Library and the internationally known Michigan Molecular Institute for polymer research.

Just a short distance away is the Chippewa Nature Center, a 1,000-acre area that includes an 1870 homestead farm, a maple-sugar house, a pioneer schoolhouse, and miles of walking trails. If you walk from the gardens to the Nature Center, you will cross the Tridge, a three-branched footbridge that links Midland's rivers.

Minnesota

SOUTHWESTERN MINNESOTA

Lake Shetek State Park (47)

Directions: The park is located 14 miles northeast of Slayton and 33 miles south of Marshall. Take Highway 59 from either community to Highway 30 and the town of Currie. Access to the park is from County Road 38, 4 miles north of Currie.

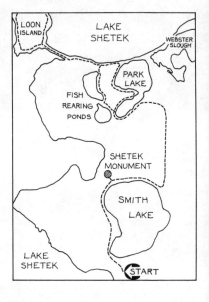

Best Season: Spring and fall.

Length: Varies; there are a number of trails in the park.

Degree of Difficulty: Easy to moderate; terrain is relatively flat.

Highlights: A variety of natural habitats, including islands, prairie, woodland marshes, and forest provide a diversity of sights, and the history of this place is fascinating.

Lake Shetek (*shetek* is the Sioux word for "pelican") is the largest lake in southwestern Minnesota and is the focal point of the 1,175-acre Lake Shetek State Park. Shoreline trails along the lake provide beautiful views, especially at dawn and sunset. Some development has occurred along the shores of Lake Shetek—cabins and some year-round homes, etc.—but there is no development around the smaller Smith Lake, which is also part of the park, and so it has remained a traditional stopping place for migratory ducks and pelicans. The best places to observe waterfowl, according to nominator Mark Crawford, are Loon Island and on the shores of Webster Slough. Mark especially likes to walk the various trails in mid-May "when the park is alive with the activities of spring. Warblers and other songbirds are at their peak migration, waterfowl are beginning to nest, wildflowers are blooming and the trails are lightly used." In the spring and fall, you may even see an eagle or two.

Several historic sites can be seen from the trails, and they act as reminders of the rich and often dramatic history of the area. The first people to come to southwestern Minnesota were wandering hunters, dependent on the herds of bison. The numerous small lakes in the area gave rise to the Indian Great Oasis Culture and later, after horses were introduced to the area by the Spanish settlers in the southwest, the Plains Culture. French fur traders arrived in the early nineteenth century and set up trading posts along the rivers and lakes. But the area remained unsettled by Europeans, mostly because the Sioux Indians were hostile and unpredictable. By the mid-1850s, however, the Sioux had been confined to two small reservations on the Minnesota River.

The situation was far from satisfactory. The Indians on the reservation were deprived of their livelihood because they were unable to hunt bison. Instead, they became totally dependent on government doles which were small or late or even nonexistent. In 1862, the Sioux revolted and attempted to drive the settlers from the Minnesota Valley. At that time Lake Shetek was the major pioneer settlement in southwestern Minnesota. Rampaging Sioux massacred twelve families in this settlement; the survivors fled. More than twenty years passed before settlers returned to the area. Today everything seems peaceful around the lake; the forests planted by the early settlers provide shelter to a variety of wildlife including deer, fox, mink, beaver, chipmunk, and squirrel. There is little indication of the tragedy that occurred here, but knowing about it increases the value of the walk. It is part of our history, and it is important to remember it.

EASTERN MINNESOTA

Duluth Skywalk (48)

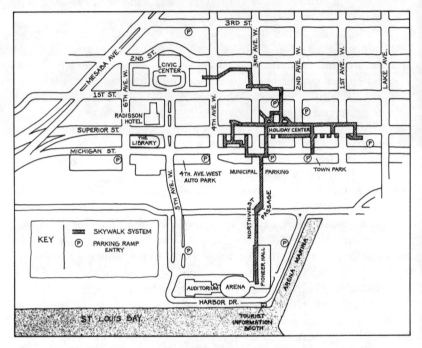

Directions: From I-35, take the Duluth downtown exit to the Holiday Center on Superior Street, where the Skywalk begins.

Best Season: Year-round.

Length: 4 miles round-trip.

Degree of Difficulty: Very easy!

Highlights: An all-year-round unique indoor hiking experience which takes the walker up and over the downtown area of the city of Duluth.

The visitor to Duluth will find a real treat in the city's climate-controlled Skywalk. Built originally to revive the downtown business district, it quickly became a popular hiking trail for young and old alike. Walkers go up and down escalators, elevators, or stairways, built to accommodate the change in elevation because the city is on a hillside, and there are wonderful views throughout because the Skywalk is mostly glass-enclosed.

This walk originates in the Holiday Center and spreads out in four segments (a fifth is in the planning stage). Robert Schadel, who nominated the Skywalk, tells us that the most interesting segment is the "northwest passage," which takes the walker over the city's main thoroughfare at a height of about fourteen feet. From there, this segment passes through the Norwest Bank Building, crosses Michigan Street, and goes on to the Arena-Auditorium, a huge complex on the waterfront. To the west is the new library, which Robert describes as "looking like a huge spaceship that has just landed." From your Skywalk vantage point, you'll have a great view of the harbor excursion boats as well as the retired iron-ore boat, the *William A. Irwin*. An aerial-lift bridge straddles the canal and connects the harbor (the largest inland harbor in the United States) with Lake Superior. In the distance you can see the city of Superior, Wisconsin, home of the world's largest grain elevators.

The Skywalk makes a loop around the Arena-Auditorium, and as you walk back you'll get an impressive view of the Duluth skyline, including the cylindrical Radisson Hotel, which is topped by a rotating restaurant. Robert suggests you take a close look at the supporting columns of the arena where you'll find pictures of Duluth's sports hall-of-famers.

The second longest segment of the Skywalk, a half mile in total, is the Mayor's Walk, which leads, of course, to City Hall. The two other segments, the Banker's Walk, which leads to the Torrey Building and the Superior Walk, which ends at the Minnesota Power Building, are both ⅜ mile long.

Before or after your skywalk, plan to spend some time at the Holiday Center. It's on four levels, all connected by glass elevators or escalators, and it includes many shops, services, and restaurants.

For a contrasting image of Duluth, take the car and drive north on Route 61, along Lake Superior to Lester Park. Take the Seven Bridges Road over old stone bridges and on up to Hawk Ridge, where you'll enjoy a panoramic view of Duluth Harbor. Next, follow Skyline Drive to the Hawk Ridge Nature Preserve where close to 71,000 hawks have been cited during their annual migration from mid-August through September.

EASTERN MINNESOTA

Duluth Western Waterfront Trail (49)

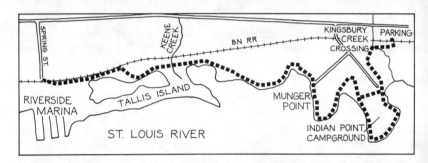

Directions: From I-35 take Highway 23 in Duluth to 71st Avenue West. Park in the parking lot across from the Lake Superior Zoological Gardens.

Best Season: Spring, but trail is open and enjoyed year-round.

Length: 5 miles round-trip; a two-hour leisurely walk.

Degree of Difficulty: Easy.

Highlights: A city walk along the water's edge.

"I sincerely believe this is one of the most delightful city walks anywhere," says nominator Robert Wentz. "You are in the city, but you feel as though you're in a wilderness."

From the parking lot, the path leads down a slight grade and crosses Kingsbury Creek, which empties into a large marsh. Here, especially in the spring, a host of waterfowl can be seen—mallards, the drakes particularly showy in their brilliant teal plumage; Canada geese; the smaller goldeneyes with their green topnotch and white cheek patch; and the buffleheads. "Whistling swans, among the most elegant and graceful of birds, also love it here," Robert says, "and you may even spot a bald eagle or two."

There are places to exercise and limber up along the first part of the trail, which was developed on an abandoned railroad right-of-way along the St. Louis River and donated to the city by the Burlington Northern Railroad. As you continue the walk, each bend in the river leads to something new or interesting to see. A muskrat, maybe, or a beaver, Indian Point Campground, a large grassy area surrounded by lovely birch, or Munger Point, named after environmentalist and State Legislator Willard Munger, whose beautiful brick and wood home looks down over the trail.

Farther on, the path crosses Keene Creek and Tallis Island, another resting place for waterfowl.

"Everybody one meets on the trail is thrilled to be there," Robert tells us. "One youngster about ten years of age was fishing with a cane pole. He was so wrapped up in watching a muskrat carry mud back and forth to build his home that he didn't notice his fishing bobber was going crazy. And an older couple I had met on the trail before came round a bend to enthusiastically share their citing of a pair of otter."

EASTERN MINNESOTA

Personal Heritage Walk (50)

Directions: Margaret Olson Webster's "personal" walk is located about 50 miles west of Duluth and can be reached via Highway 210 between Wright and Tamarack on County Road 22.

Best Season: Year-round.

Length: The walk takes about three-quarters of an hour, but it might be longer depending on the people you meet and the number of side trips you want to take.

Degree of Difficulty: Easy.

Highlights: On this scenic walk you are never out of sight of a lake or a tree. But what nominator Margaret Webster likes best about it is the opportunity it gives her to "walk in the footsteps of her forebears." She hopes this walk will inspire you to find your own personal heritage walk.

We thought the idea of a "heritage walk" was so unique and interesting that we decided to include it, and because Margaret Webster's personal walk is just some fifty miles west of Duluth, it may be that you will be able to share it with her some day. The area is lovely, dotted with the numerous glacial lakes that give Minnesota its nickname of "Land of 10,000 Lakes."

"Walking is, among other positive things, a time to get in touch with ourselves, in body, mind, and soul," writes Margaret. "A superior way to do this is to walk the same paths as our ancestors did. A walk which takes us back to the pathways followed by our hardy ancestors can open new paths to discovering more about ourselves and them.

"Because of the vast, relatively unchanged rural areas in the midwest, many midwesterners will find it relatively easy to return to 'root' locations and to rediscover those paths trod by their ancestors.

"The experience can be deep, even across oceans. My daughter had an opportunity to walk family land in Finland, and she felt a bond which was hard for her to explain, one that could not have been experienced in any other way!

"Talk with family members, read old letters, and research newspapers, books, and other references to help you locate your own personal heritage walk."

Perhaps when you do take your own heritage walk you will be inspired as Margaret was to write a poem about it. We share hers with you here:

"WALKING IS MY HERITAGE"

Walking is my heritage
My route...one that has been well walked before me,
This unpaved narrow country lane has borne the weight
Of many moods and modes of errands.

The sweet pungent smoke
Which has curled up from the Walli sauna
Through dusk for nearly a hundred years
Puts me in touch with my world, now and then.

Yeasty, the smell of the earth
Is good as it rises after the rain, rich and real.
Birch, aspen, pine, maple and oak. Tamarack, sumac
Swampgrass, cattail and wild rose grow as if forever.

The Hannuri Ghost House
Home of the local Katilo,
Who handled births and medical needs
As she saw fit, flamboyant,
Not caring how others evalued behavior.

Proud old white schoolhouse
Scene of a new language struggle, books and chalk,
Funerals, parties, war projects, dances and talks: Whose
Large long windows turn to gold in the setting sun.

Mother, were windows gold
As you spritely hiked to dance or spelling bee?
Or hurried home with pails of berries, or turned the corner
In the flivver of your new suitor?

Uncle Ted in his pickup...
Saw more on this road than I hope to. Numbered the trees
Knew when one rabbit visited another. Never before so still
In granite garden. The end of his walk and mine.

The wide gold band on my finger
Links me with his mother. She traveled this road,
My grandmother, offering life and love and service,
Sharing her skills and her songs.

Now I walk this road for my life:
What will it mean to others that I've moved this gravel,
If ever so slightly in my daily journey?
Walking is my heritage.

SOUTHEASTERN MINNESOTA

Minneapolis: Minnehaha Falls (51)

Directions: The walk is located in Minnehaha Park, off Route 55 in south Minneapolis. You can drive your own car or take public transportation (bus or taxi) to the park.

Best Season: Late spring, summer, early fall.

Length: 1 mile from the falls to the Mississippi River and back.

Degree of Difficulty: Easy.

Highlights: A great walk in a setting not usually found in a city.

From the waterfall he named her, Minnehaha, Laughing Water.

On this walk you'll have a chance to see the waterfall Henry Wadsworth Longfellow immortalized in "The Song of Hiawatha," but never actually saw. Instead, the poet, who wrote "Hiawatha" in 1855, relied on the reports of those who had been there: explorers, missionaries, fur traders.

Today the 53-foot waterfall is a favorite place of both locals and visitors alike. Jean Otteson, who nominated the walk, likes it especially after a rainfall because that's when it is most powerful and exciting. A path leads up close to the falls so you can experience this power firsthand.

From the falls, walk along the path that leads to the Mississippi

River. This is a quiet place, shared by squirrels, chipmunks, birds, and wildflowers. When you reach the river, you can sit on one of the boulders and view the comings and goings on the water. There's lots to see, and it's a great place for a picnic.

Return to the falls via the bridge at the end of the Minnehaha Creek and walk upstream a short distance to the statue of Hiawatha carrying Minnehaha across the falls. Minneapolis schoolchildren donated their pennies to make this statue possible.

A footbridge just above the falls leads to Minnehaha Depot which was built in 1870 as a stop on the Milwaukee Railroad's Chicago-Minneapolis run. Nearby is the John Stevens House, the first wood-frame house built in Minneapolis. There are 144 acres in Minnehaha Park, so plan to spend some time exploring this lovely place.

Before or after you visit the park, nominator Jean Otteson recommends a walk around Nicollet Mall in Minneapolis. Park at the Lock and Dam Observatory near Portland Avenue and Second Street. "Nicollet Mall," explains Jean, "is a twelve-block pedestrian mall where cars are not allowed." (Buses and taxis are available.) Two of the favorite sites are the IDS (Investors Diversified Services) Building, a 57-story edifice with a crystal court, mirrorlike exterior, and, from the top, a superb view of Minneapolis (lakes included), and the Conservatory, a new shopping center built from glass and marble imported from Europe. "It's touted as a unique European shopping experience," says Jean, who enjoys the mall best at Christmastime when it is decorated with festive banners, wreaths, and lights.

SOUTHEASTERN MINNESOTA

St. Paul Skyway System (52)

Directions: From I-94, exit on Tenth Street; from I-35E, exit on Wacouta Street. Head for the central business district of St. Paul.

Best Season: This is an indoor walk for all seasons.

Length: 3.75 miles.

Degree of Difficulty: Easy, but slight grade changes and stairways offer opportunities for those seeking a more strenuous walk.

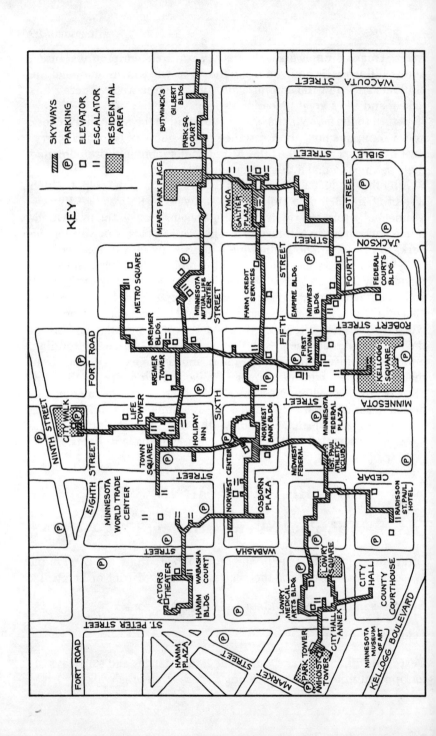

Highlights: A delightful jaunt on St. Paul's indoor walkway that's protected from the weather and full of surprises.

According to nominator William A. Buth, Minnesota's capital city is home to the largest publicly owned walkway in the United States. Called the St. Paul Skyway System, this unique walking experience allows you to view such things as St. Paul's historic district, the Federal Courts Building, and the Minnesota World Trade Center—all from a comfortable climate-controlled environment.

If you come in winter, there may be snowdrifts visible outside, but you'll be warm as toast as you enjoy the holiday spirit that pervades the Skyway. Young and old alike share in the festivities which include a Winter Carnival Skyway Parade. In fact, throughout the year there are numerous Skyway events: running and walking marathons and a variety of entertainment. For residents, the Skyway represents a sort of city park to be enjoyed year-round.

Added to all this is the convenience of shopping, banking, and, eating. William Buth sums up this fascinating walk perfectly: "At any time of year, a given walker will be subjected to various sights, aromas of fresh popcorn or coffee, and changing vistas which provide a kaleidoscope of points of interest. The St. Paul Skyway is considered by many to be a 3.75-mile-long town hall where greetings are exchanged and business conducted, and where leisurely strolls exercise both mind and muscle."

NORTHEASTERN MINNESOTA

Superior Hiking Trail (53)

Directions: The trail is located in the Sawtooth Mountains above the north shore of Lake Superior, ninety minutes northeast of Duluth. Take I-61 to the village of Tofte; the walk begins at the Bluefin Bay Resort.

Best Season: April and May; November.

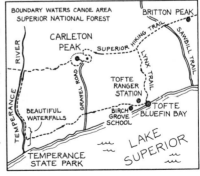

Length: 13 miles round-trip (but you can hike for days in this area).

Degree of Difficulty: Easy to moderately difficult.

Highlights: An invigorating walk with a superb vista of Lake Superior.

Lake Superior is the largest body of fresh water in the world, encompassing some 32,000 square miles. This walk begins in Tofte, one of the towns along the lake. Founded in 1890 by Norwegians John and Andrew Tofte, it became an important logging and fishing settlement. Today Tofte is more or less a "gateway" to the Sawtooth Mountains and to the delights of Lake Superior.

Robert Buntz, Jr., of St. Paul, who nominated this walk, tells us that one of the great features of the entire Lake Superior Trail System is that you can gain access to it from many of the resorts along the northern shore of the lake. A series of loop trails gives you the opportunity to spend days hiking new routes and yet always have a place to come back to at night. This particular 13-mile walk begins at the Bluefin Bay Resort. Robert describes it for us:

"It was a crisp day in November when Mary and I struck off on the new Superior Hiking Trail heading north from Bluefin Bay out of Tofte. The first mile and a half of our 13-mile trek was a moderate uphill grade—just enough to get the blood flowing and the body warm. In fact, midway up we shed our jackets and walked along in sweaters only.

"After leaving the village of Tofte we were immediately in the forest, walking a well-marked trail. Passing over a small stream, we soon came to a beaver dam and pond from which we could see Carleton Peak (the highest point on the north shore, rising 1,529 feet above the lake). We continued on our way to the sounds of birds calling their greetings and warnings. Soon we came across the Superior Hiking Trail and headed west to Carleton.

"The stretch from the Bluefin Access Trail to Carleton is a relatively flat one, crossing small streams or wet areas (on footbridges) and passing through lots of open space and low bush. It was very quiet. At the end of this part, we started up the back side (north) of Carleton Peak.

"This upward portion is moderate in grade with a few fairly difficult spots. Here we encountered the only other person we saw on the trail. His only comment was, 'It's a bit steep at the top, but well worth it.' He was right. There's about a 50-yard section near the top which would be difficult for the average walker. The reward, however, is great. Upon attaining the summit, we were thrilled. We really felt as though we had gone far away. The vista of Lake Superior was spectacular.

"After soaking up the view and the feeling of peacefulness, we proceeded down the peak and walked west to the Temperance River. This is truly one of the most scenic rivers in the midwest. Our walk took us south along the river toward the big lake. As we got closer to civilization, and the powerful cascades, we could read about the geologic history of the gorge on placards along the trail. It was fascinating.

"After enjoying the power of the river, we started back east along a trail paralleling Highway 61, but far-enough removed to feel remote. The 4 miles back to Bluefin along this trail seemed like a leisurely stroll after the sometimes rigorous hike up the mountain and back down to the river. It was a great way to end the walk."

Missouri

WESTERN MISSOURI

Kansas City: Plaza Walking Art Tour (54)

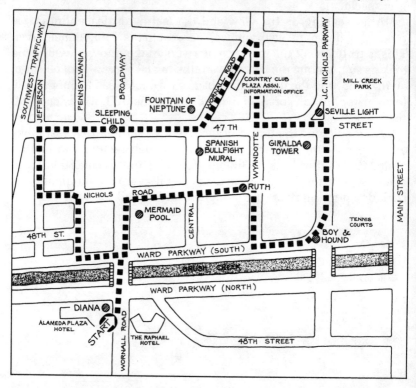

Directions: The walk takes place in the Country Club Plaza, located 5 miles south of downtown Kansas City.

Best Season: Year-round.

Length: Under 2 miles, but you could spend all day in this outdoor fantasyland.

Degree of Difficulty: Easy.

Highlights: Spectacular works of art from all over the world in an outdoor setting.

This is a truly unique walk which affords an opportunity to see a collection of art that has taken nearly seventy years to put together. From towers to fountains to sculptures to a court of penguins, the Plaza Walking Art Tour is a tour de force which includes spectacular art from Italy, Spain, England, Greece, and other areas of Europe. Of special interest are the magnificent Italian sculptures of Carrara marble—the statue of *Ruth*, for example, by Pasquale Romanelli, and the mermaid pool, believed to have been created around 1680. You will be impressed by the diversity of art found here. A beautiful Bernard Zuckermann sculpture of *Diana* stands in front of one of the largest artificially constructed waterfalls in America, and a huge ceramic mural from Seville, depicting a Spanish bullfight, decorates an entire wall. Nominator Beverly Metzger tells us that "a favorite spot in the park is the fountain in Chandler Court with the statue of *Pan* and his forest domain keeping watch over the passersby. And thousands of good luck wishes have been rubbed from the nose of the bronze *Boar* statue and fountain. All the money dropped in this fountain goes to local charities."

Beverly also recommends a close look at a more contemporary statue, *Out to Lunch*, which depicts a small boy reading a book while eating a hamburger. And where is this enchanting work of bronze located? "In front of McDonald's hamburgers, of course," replies Beverly. For a self-guided brochure of the artwork in the plaza, stop in at the Plaza Merchant's Association, 4625 Wornall Road.

Often referred to as America's Original Shopping District, the plaza was developed in 1922. Today it embraces more than 55 acres and is a wonderful example of the successful atmosphere that can be created by a blending of art with commercial endeavors. You can do just about anything in the plaza—eat, sleep, drink, get your hair cut, go to the movies, see your banker, or do nothing at all. You can sit and enjoy watching the people, stroll past some of the world's greatest works of art, or listen to free concerts featuring the Kansas City Symphony or any number of well-known big band, country, and rock musicians. "The walker will want to plan on spending a lot of time here," says Beverly, "because it's an unforgettable atmosphere of outdoor treasures."

WESTERN MISSOURI

Kansas City: Penn Valley Park (55)

Directions: Penn Valley Park is located twelve blocks due south of the downtown area. Best access to the towering Liberty Memorial is Main Street to 26th Street to Memorial Drive.

Best Season: Year-round.

Length: Just over 1 mile.

Degree of Difficulty: Easy; the 1-mile paved course on the crest of a hill is level.

Highlights: Magnificent views of the city from a tranquil park setting.

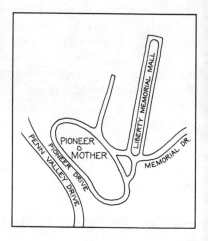

The Penn Valley Park Walking and Jogging Trail was opened in 1986 and passes by the impressive Liberty Memorial, a 217-foot monument dedicated to World War I, and the Liberty Memorial Museum, the only museum in the country solely dedicated to World War I. Nominator Gary Maun says that "framed behind the Memorial is one of the most impressive scenes of the downtown Kansas City skyline, located about a dozen blocks to the north." In fact, the entire trail runs along the crest of a high hill, offering the best views of the city anywhere.

The trees lining Liberty Memorial Drive were planted years ago in honor of local war casualties, and many have markers at the base. This very moving tribute is spectacular in the fall when the leaves display a vivid show of colors.

The trail winds around a grassy park area and leads to a statue called *Pioneer Mother*. This large work of art depicts three frontiersmen and a pioneer woman with a baby in her arms crossing the wilderness on horseback. The statue, which lies in the path of the old pioneer route from the Missouri River to the settlement of Westport, is dedicated to the thousands of women who set out on unknown trails leading west. Westport, the outpost for the Santa Fe Trail, is just 4 miles from downtown Kansas City.

Also nearby is another statue commemorating westward expansion, that of the *Indian Scout*, and a third statue dedicated to the doughboys of World War I.

"Walkers will feel as if they're part of a picture postcard," Gary says. "This walk offers the best of urbanity and tranquility."

WESTERN MISSOURI

Independence: Harry S Truman Historic District (56)

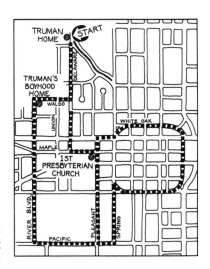

Directions: The walk begins at the Truman home, 219 North Delaware Street.

Best Season: Year-round.

Length: 1 mile.

Degree of Difficulty: Easy.

Highlights: A walk in the footsteps of President Truman.

This walk begins at the Truman home, a grand white Victorian, built in 1867 and full of history. It was here, for example, that Secretary of State Dean Acheson informed Truman of the invasion of South Korea on June 24, 1950.

Many notable homes can be seen along this walk, including that of Charles S. Thomas, Secretary of the Navy from 1954 to 1957; Truman's boyhood home at the corner of River Boulevard and Waldo Avenue, and the high school from which both Harry and Bess Truman graduated. A tour brochure notes that "one of Mr. Truman's teachers, upon presenting one of his classmates with a kiss, told the future President that he would get a kiss when he did something notable. Harry Truman never forgot this occasion, and many years later would recall its significance."

In addition to picturesque homes, nominator Karen Johannesmeyer tells us that many of the buildings along the walk are unique in architectural design. Among these are the Gothic-style First Presbyterian Church which Truman attended, and the Memorial Building across the street, which served as Truman's polling grounds during the elections.

The town of Independence is itself a tribute to the common sense and strength of character of the thirty-third president of the United States, and the people of Independence are determined to keep it that way. The sidewalks and roads are lined with trees, and a sense of respect for the past parades the community. Truman's biographer, Jonathan Daniels, has said that "Truman the man matches the sturdy midwestern character of North Delaware Street and the neighborhood which more than any other suggests the life and career of the former Chief Executive."

As you travel these streets of Independence, imagine yourself walking alongside Harry S Truman, who was also an enthusiastic walker. Of course, you'll have to walk fast to keep up with him. As Karen Johannesmeyer reminds us, Truman believed that to make a walk count, it should be done "as if you are going somewhere."

EASTERN MISSOURI

Sainte Genevieve (57)

Directions: Sainte Genevieve is located about 60 miles south of St. Louis on U.S. 61 (I-55). The walk begins at the corner of Fourth and Merchant streets.

Best Season: Year-round.

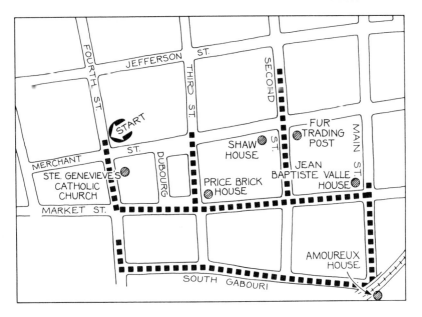

Length: Just several city blocks, but allow at least half a day to enjoy Sainte Genevieve.

Degree of Difficulty: Easy.

Highlights: A chance to walk through the first permanent settlement in Missouri and discover history "off the beaten track."

This walk was nominated by Catharine Smith, who visited Sainte Genevieve ten years ago and has never forgotten it. Unlike restored villages such as those found in Williamsburg, Virginia, or Plymouth, Massachusetts, the residents of Sainte Genevieve are, for the most part, still using the structures erected in the eighteenth and nineteenth centuries as private homes and businesses.

Founded by the French in about 1725, Sainte Genevieve was the first settlement on the west bank of the Mississippi River. Residents and visitors to the town, known as the "Mother of the West," include artist-naturalist Jean Jacques Audubon; Moses Austin, the "founder" of Texas; Otto the First, King of Greece; and, according to legend, Lafayette and Jesse James.

The town's French heritage is celebrated every New Year's Eve when revelers sing and dance "La Guignolee," an old French song, and during the second week in August at the festival called *Jour du Fête*. Evidence of its French history can also be found in Sainte Genevieve's restaurants where such foods as *bouillon*, a hearty chicken-vegetable soup, and *andouille*, a spicy homemade sausage, are served. You can almost trace the history of the town's residents by sampling the food in the various restaurants. Peppery port steaks, for example, proclaim a Spanish heritage, and smoked beef sausage, now known as Sainte Genevieve sausage, is a legacy from the German butcher who came to town in the early nineteenth century.

First stop on this walking tour is the Sainte Genevieve Catholic Church at Fourth and Merchant streets. The Price Brick House, believed to be the oldest brick building west of the Mississippi, is located at Third and Market streets. Furnished as it would have been in the 1800s, it is today a restaurant and tavern.

Walk down Market and turn left on Second Street. As you approach Merchant Street again, you'll find Shaw House, with its doors from an early steamboat and the Fur Trading Post with slave quarters, where there are several museum displays.

Go back to Market Street and turn left on Main, where you'll find the Jean Baptiste Valle House. Built in the 1780s, this was the seat of the American government after the Louisiana Purchase. The original one-and-a-half-story house has been modified by the addition of a second floor. The home is occupied and not open to the public.

Cross Market on Main Street and visit the Bolduc–Le Meilleur House and the Bolduc House. The latter is especially interesting because it is the first instance of an authentic French Colonial house in the Mississippi Valley being put back in its original form. Across the street is Beauvais House, which was built in the 1770s.

Now, walk back down Main and cross South Gabouri Street for the pièce de résistance of the walk—Amoureux House. Built in about 1770, this wonderful Creole residence has its original hip-roof framing, massive Norman trusses, and a huge walnut mantel.

Following your walk through Sainte Genevieve, you may want to spend some time by the Mississippi where fishing and boating is available, or at Pere Marquette City Park, 52 acres of greenery on the north edge of town.

EASTERN MISSOURI

Berryman Trail (58)

Directions: The walk is located in the Potosi Ranger District of the Mark Twain National Forest. From St. Louis, take I-55 to Festus and pick up Route 21 south to Potosi. The Trailhead is 17 miles west of Potosi on Route 8, then turn north (right)1 mile on Forest Road 2266. You can also reach the trail by taking I-44 west out of St. Louis to the Bourbon exit. At Bourbon, head south on Country Route N and drive for 13 miles to the intersection with Route W. Head south on W for 10 miles to the Brazil Creek Campground on the Berryman Trail.

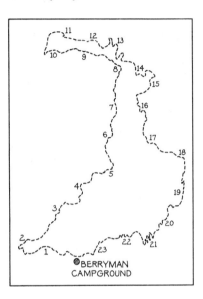

Best Season: Spring and fall.

Length: 24 miles. (Numbers on map signify mileage.)

Degree of Difficulty: Moderate; there are some small hills.

Highlights: A long scenic trail with lots of places to stop and camp or picnic.

This loop trail, which passes by the Berryman Campground, winds through forests of oak, pine, and stream bottom hardwoods, then climbs to high rocky ridges. A few open areas alternate with the forest to provide a diverse array of flora and fauna.

At the Berryman Campground, which was originally a Civilian Conservation Corps camp, there are eight camping units and four picnic areas. There are no developed drinking water sources along the trail, but there are camping and picnic sites approximately every 5 or 6 miles, giving the hiker plenty of options as to where to stop and rest, either for a few hours or for the night. Overnight camping is allowed anywhere along the trail route.

"The woods are particularly beautiful in spring or fall," says nominator John Woerheide, "spring for the dogwoods, fall for the colorful foliage." Roads intersect the trail at various points, and John suggests that you arrange to leave another car at one of these intersections or have someone pick you up, if you don't want to hike the entire trail.

When you've finished your walk on the Berryman Trail and your exploration of the Mark Twain National Forest, you can hop back into the car and drive to Elephant Rocks State Park, south of Potosi on Route 21, just north of the town of Graniteville. Here you can see dramatic outcroppings of granite. The huge rounded boulders are actually igneous rock more than a billion years old. From the parking lot, you can take a 1-mile walk that circles the rocks. There are explanations along the trail to help you understand how these curious formations came to be.

EASTERN MISSOURI

Ellisville: Year-Round Event Walk (59)

Directions: Ellisville is located near the Missouri River, southwest of St. Louis. Head south on Highway 340 (Clarkson Road) from Highway 40 (I-64). Continue on to Ellisville. The walk begins in the Clarkson/Clayton Shopping Center, at Dierbergs Market.

Best Season: Year-round.

Length: 7 miles; allow two to four hours, depending on pace.

Degree of Difficulty: Mostly easy. There are some moderate slopes and one set of stairs.

Highlights: Rural and suburban environments contrast nicely on this walk through seven city parks.

Designed as a "Volkssport event," this walk was enjoyed by more than 1,000 walkers during its first nine months of existence. Every-

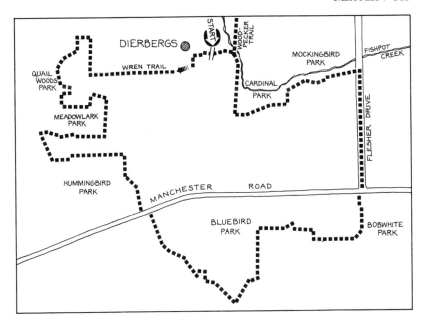

one who has experienced it enthusiastically proclaims it "the best." Dr. Perry Rawson, President of the Lions Volkssport Club, has walked it more than sixteen times since its opening in 1986. "This walk has been the single most important means for me to continue distance credit during the significantly long quiet periods of Volksmarch activity in the area," he says. So all you Volkssport enthusiasts take note.

But this is not just for "Volkssporters." This is a walk for everyone. There's no competition and you can go at your own pace: The whole family, from the smallest child to the eldest grandparent, can participate.

Donald Essen, who nominated the Ellisville walk, calls it "a walk for all seasons, a showcase for Missouri's contrasting weather. Springtime shows the earth bursting forth in bloom and bud as flora and fauna awake from winter's sleep. Walkers hiking the trail on hot summer days receive respite from the sun's rays as full-leafed mature trees provide many high-canopied glades. Few places in the world compete with the fall color display put on by the various hardwood forests in the Ellisville parks. When winter comes and the denuded trees stand sentinel, beautiful snows blanket the forests with tranquil pristine beauty."

The walk begins and ends in the Clarkson/Clayton Shopping Center where you can browse to your heart's content alongside local shoppers. From there, you'll move on to the Wren Trail, which passes by the Daniel Boone County Library branch and through several residential areas. You'll visit Quail Woods Park and walk by the Ellisville City Hall. Once you have crossed Manchester Road, you'll pass under one of the few covered bridges in west St. Louis County to the 175-acre Bluebird Park, where all sorts of people are sure to be enjoying themselves in numerous outdoor activities. In all, you'll visit seven parks, each one named for a Missouri bird.

From Bluebird Park, the trail leads through the forest to Bobwhite Park and then back to Manchester Road, where, if you're hungry, you can stop for a bite to eat in one of the many restaurants.

Head north across Manchester and down Flesher Drive to Fishpot Creek. Follow the winding course of the floodplain, and cross the creek to the Woodpecker Trail section, which crosses another bridge and eventually leads back to the shopping center. If you're a Volksmarcher, be sure to get your book validated at Dierbergs Market.

In conclusion Don Essen says: "The entire walk is a unique, unforgettable experience."

SOUTHERN MISSOURI

Lake of the Ozarks:
Walk of the Four Seasons (60)

Directions: The walk is located just north of Osage Beach in Lake Ozark. Once in Lake Ozark, take Business Route 54 to HH to Bittersweet, then go ¼ mile to the Start sign where the walk begins.

Best Season: Spring, when the dogwoods are in bloom, or fall, when the leaves change color.

Length: 6.2 miles; the time varies.

Degree of Difficulty: Moderately difficult because of rolling terrain.

Highlights: A scenic, challenging walk through the colorful peaceful woods around the beautiful Lake of the Ozarks.

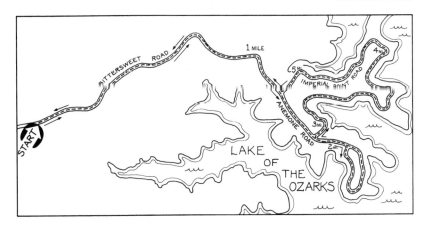

Lake of the Ozarks is the happy result of Bagnell Dam, which was constructed on the Osage River in 1931 in order to produce electric power. With more than 1,300 miles of shoreline, the lake winds through the Osage River Valley providing an exquisite area of natural beauty which has become Missouri's largest and most popular resort area.

Marianne Bushman McClaughry, who nominated this Walk of the Four Seasons, says that the course was developed for running and walking competitions and is certified by The Athletic Congress (TAC). But Marianne likes to walk it just for fun and exercise. "The experience is enhanced tremendously by the natural beauty surrounding this course," she says. "Frequently during an early morning or a twilight walk I come across deer, occasionally a wild turkey, and always squirrels, birds, and other interesting flora and fauna."

Oak, dogwood, maple, and birch trees, as well as wildflowers of every hue and color, line the course which overlooks the lake. There are also the intriguing Indian Thong trees which Marianne says were used as a means of communication by the Osage Indians. The Indians would bend the saplings so they would point in a specific direction— toward water, for example, or toward a village.

The course offers wonderful views of natural beauty. Further, the lovely landscape is enhanced by luxurious resort homes which stand majestically along the shoreline and by sailboats, water-skiers, and cruisers which dot the lake. As an added plus, this walk will give you a chance to meet some interesting folk: top-level executives, for example, taking the walk to relax; retirees eager for a chance to share years of experiences; vacationers from all over the world.

CENTRAL MISSOURI

Jefferson City: A Walk through the Past (61)

Directions: Missouri's capital is located at the juncture of Routes 50 and 63 in the heart of the state.

Best Season: Year-round.

Length: 1.5 miles, but it's a good idea to allow half a day for this walk through history.

Degree of Difficulty: Easy.

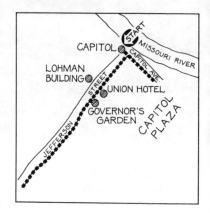

Highlights: The magnificent state capitol, which stands on a limestone bluff and is visible from almost every corner of the city, is the spiritual and physical highlight of this walk.

The walk begins at the Missouri Capitol, which overlooks the Missouri River on Capitol Avenue. The building, constructed in 1911 after a fire destroyed the original capitol, covers three acres. The first floor houses two museums of historic interest. Note the large state seal in the first-floor rotunda which is wrought in bronze. On the capitol grounds stands a bronze relief depicting the signing of the Louisiana Purchase. Nominator Marlene Asel says that if you take this walk on Monday, Tuesday, or Thursday when the legislature is in session, you are invited to watch from the Visitors' Gallery.

Next on the walk is the Lohman Building on Jefferson Street, one of three buildings you'll pass on what is known as Jefferson Landing. This area was restored during Missouri's bicentennial celebration. Built in the 1830s, the Lohman Building is thought to be the oldest in Jefferson City. From about 1850 to 1870, the building was used as an inn, store, and warehouse where steamboat passengers could find lodging and a wide variety of items for purchase.

Across from the Lohman Building is the Union Hotel, which was built in the 1850s, and next to that is the Governor's Garden, which was completed in the late 1930s as part of the WPA program to combat unemployment during the depression. Walkways lead through the garden, which is open to the public. The Governor's Residence was built in 1871. Inside there's an elegant winding stairway, and magnificent marble fireplaces can be seen in many of the rooms.

Tours of the home are conducted every Tuesday, and during the first weekend in December, there's a candlelight tour, at which time the governor and his wife greet each guest personally. There is also an annual Christmas parade held during this weekend, with floats, bands, and, of course, Santa Claus. "The Governor's Residence is always decorated beautifully for the holidays, and it's a fun time to be here," according to Marlene. For more information about the candlelight tour, call (314) 751-4141.

From the Governor's Residence, the walk takes you past the Cole County Historical Museum, several other homes and historic buildings, and ends on the other side of Capitol Plaza at the statue of *Thomas Jefferson* for whom the city was named. Over thirteen feet tall, the statue stands at the center of the stairway leading to the huge bronze doors of the capitol.

"Jefferson City has a warm, homey atmosphere to it," Marlene tells us. "It's full of history, rich in hospitality, and abundant with possibilities."

Nebraska

NORTHWESTERN NEBRASKA

Trooper Trail (62)

Directions: The trail is located in Soldier Creek Wood Reserve which adjoins the largest state park in Nebraska, Fort Robinson. From Crawford, take Highway 20 west to Soldier Creek Military Road. Turn right and follow signs to the east gate.

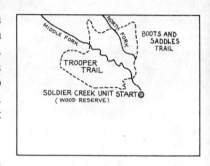

Best Season: Spring, fall, summer.

Length: 8 miles; allow about two-and-a-half hours.

Degree of Difficulty: Moderately easy.

Highlights: Scenic walk with views of the Badlands on historic trails of the Old West.

The trail begins at the east gate of Soldier Creek Wood Reserve where three creek beds meet. It proceeds west, then branches north, joining parts of the Boots and Saddles Trail as it slices its way through the reserve and heads up to a high ridge where you can see the Badlands. If you've never seen the Badlands before, you are in for a surprise. "It's like being on the moon," says nominator Vince Rotherham. "There is no vegetation, and the land is uneven due to wind and rain and erosion."

From here the trail goes east for about ¾ mile where it crosses the North Fork and heads south, back to the beginning. If you want a longer hike, go on across the South Creek (Vince recommends you take a drink from any of the spring-fed creeks in the reserve) and continue west in a loop, which will bring you back to Trooper Trail.

This trail, as well as others in the reserve, has been in existence for hundreds of years. Long before your sneakers or hiking shoes left their mark, the trail had felt first the tread of soft deerskin moccasins, then the harder stomp of soldiers' boots. You may not be able to see evidence of these early walkers, but you may be able to notice the ruts left by wooden stagecoach wheels.

Nearby Fort Robinson can provide days of adventure for the whole family, with all-day hikes as well as overnight hiking trails. A two-night trail links the trails of Fort Robinson with those of Soldier Creek Wood Reserve. It follows the first 7 miles of Spring Creek Trail before connecting with the Wood Reserve Trail at an old windmill site on the west side of the loop.

In addition to walking, Fort Robinson holds a number of other attractions, including museums where you can immerse yourself in the history of the fort and of the Indian Wars of the 1870s and 1880s (the guardhouse where Crazy Horse was killed has been restored). There are also several tours, including the Fort Robinson Express, and stagecoach and buckboard rides along the old trails.

NORTHWESTERN NEBRASKA

Pine Ridge Trail (63)

Directions: The trail is located in Chadron State Park and the Pine Ridge Division of the Nebraska National Forest. From Chadron, take U.S. Highway 385 south for about 8 miles. The park entrance is well marked.

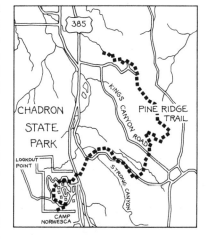

Best Season: Summer and fall for hiking; in the winter the park is wonderful for cross-country skiing.

Length: Pine Ridge Trail connects with other trails for a total of 25 miles, but you can hike various portions—it's all up to you.

Degree of Difficulty: Moderate to moderately difficult. The trail is ungroomed and is slippery when wet. Inexperienced walkers should stay on the marked trail and nominator Deb Cottier cautions that in spring there are many ticks.

Highlights: Gorgeous scenery and an abundance of wildlife.

This picturesque trail, dominated by ponderosa pines that can rise to as high as 60 feet, winds through the 860-acre Chadron State Park, the oldest in Nebraska. Here, the rugged country, with its ridges, buttes, and streams, contains a great diversity of plant and animal life. Squirrels, deer, and rabbits are commonly seen along the trail, and the more patient walker may also see wild turkeys, bobcats, raccoons, porcupines, coyotes, and even bats as it gets dark. Hawks and turkey vultures soar overhead, as well as the golden eagle.

The Pine Ridge Trail in Chadron State Park crosses the highway to the 51,000-acre Nebraska National Forest and connects with other trailheads, so it is possible to extend this walk for a total of 25 miles. All trails are well marked and easy to follow.

The area, a favorite hunting and camping grounds of the Sioux Indians, was also important as a fur trading center, first to the Spaniards from New Mexico and later to the white settlers who set up two competing trading posts. A replica of one of these posts can be seen at the Museum of the Fur Trade (open during the summer months or by appointment), east of Chadron. Here you can see the trading goods, weapons, and fur pelts that were at the root of this thriving, but dangerous business. The Bordeaux Trading Post was established in 1841 by the American Fur Company which abandoned it in 1849. It remained an independent trading post until August 1876, when the U.S. cavalry confiscated weapons that were being sold to Indians from the same tribe as those who had met and defeated General Custer and his men at The Little Bighorn just weeks before.

The other trading post was built in 1841 and operated by Louis B. Chartran until 1845 when the owners, the Sibille and Adams Fur Trading Company, sold out. Chartran, of French-Canadian ancestry, was well-respected for his good relationship with the Sioux. He married a Sioux and spent the last years of his life with them. Today his name, changed over the years to "Chadron," is borne by a town, a creek, and a state park—a reminder, perhaps, that it was possible in those times for red and white men to live peacefully together.

The area's fur trading heritage is celebrated annually on the weekend after July 4th. During these festive Chadron Fur Trade Days, there are parades, a flea market, barbecues, contests, and a "World Championship Buffalo Chip Throw." For more information, write: Chadron State Park, Chadron, NE, 69337, phone (308) 432-2036; or the Chadron Area Chamber of Commerce, P.O. Box 646, Chadron, NE, 69337, phone (308) 432-4401.

EASTERN NEBRASKA

Rock Bluff Run (64)

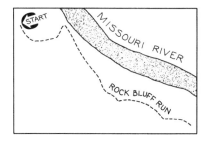

Directions: The walk is located in Indian Cave State Park. From Omaha, take I-29 to Highway 136 west. Exit at Route 67 and head south to Route 64 east, which leads into the park. Leave your car at St. Deroin School.

Best Season: Spring and fall.

Length: 5 miles round-trip.

Degree of Difficulty: Easy.

Highlights: Scenic trail with superb view of the Missouri River.

As you begin this trail you will go downhill for about a half mile and then begin a slight climb to a ridge which rises only about 300 feet. There's a bench at the top where you can rest amid Nebraska's only hardwood forest. "It's very beautiful," says nominator Larry Cook, "with a variety of oaks and hickories, ash, walnut, and other trees."

One word of caution: Timber rattlesnakes have been seen at Indian Cave. You may want to carry a snakebite kit with you, even though the chances are slim that you will meet up with one of these reptiles. If you do, you'll be glad you were prepared.

Spring is particularly beautiful at Indian Cave when the forest floor is covered with wildflowers, including phlox, mayapple, columbine, Dutchman's-breeches and lady's slipper orchids. Fall, of course, is beautiful as well, bursting with deep reds and yellows as the leaves turn.

From the bench on the ridge, the trail continues another half mile to a scenic overlook high above the Missouri River. There's a bench here, too, where you can relax and enjoy the dazzling view before descending through a meadow and heading back the way you came.

If you prefer to return via another route instead of retracing your steps, you can link up with interconnecting trails or take the road back to your car. Check in at park headquarters before you begin the walk for information on the various other trails.

EASTERN NEBRASKA

Lincoln's Year-Round Walking Event (65)

Directions: The walk begins and ends at the Cornhusker Hotel at 333 S. 13th Street in Lincoln.

Best Season: Year-round.

Length: 10 kilometers (6.2 miles); about two hours, but allow more time to visit places of interest along the way.

Degree of Difficulty: Easy, can be done with a stroller or in a wheelchair.

Highlights: Haymarket Square, city parks, art galleries, a children's zoo, and the University of Nebraska campus are just a few of the highlights of this walk, which can earn the registered walker who completes it an award.

This is a walk with an interesting history and purpose. It can be enjoyed by anyone at anytime, but it was created by the Lincoln Volkssport Club as a year-round walking event. This means that if you complete the walk (at your own pace), you can get an award at the end.

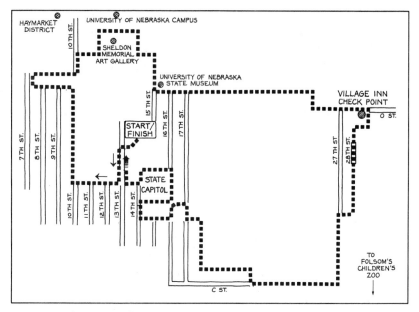

You must be properly registered, however, and you can do that easily at the start of the walk. Volkssporting, which includes biking, walking, cross-country skiing, and swimming, has been going on for years in Europe, but it is a relatively new—and growing—phenomenon in the United States. Volkssport events are noncompetitive, and the whole family can participate.

This particular walk is interesting and varied. It will take you through such areas as the historic Haymarket district, which was a lively trading area in the late 1800s, and the University of Nebraska Campus, the cultural nucleus of the city. You can stop at the Sheldon Memorial Art Gallery, which houses more than 3,000 works of art, focusing primarily on twentieth-century American art, and which offers 30 changing annual exhibits. At the University of Nebraska State Museum, you can see one of the best collections of modern and fossil elephants in the world and visit a hands-on Encounter Center where you are encouraged to touch everything. Folsom's Children's Zoo boasts the bear from *Grizzly Adams* as well as a unique child-size replica of an 1890s Nebraska town.

Teresa Boes, who nominated this walk, was present at its inauguration. She shared her experience with us:

"On January 9, 1988, the Lincoln Volkssport Club christened its new Year-Round Walking Event with about sixty participants. The day was sunny, but the temperature was only three or four degrees [above zero]. Everyone was so bundled up that sometimes we didn't recognize each other. However, leading off the walk was Nebraska Governor Kay Orr. She set a brisk pace, and invited some of the walkers back to the Governor's Mansion for hot chocolate after the walk."

Teresa has taken the walk many times since then. She's met people from Minnesota, Iowa, South Dakota, Kansas, and Wyoming. "It is not unusual for people to plan vacations or other trips so that they can participate in Volkswalks nationwide," she says. "With Lincoln so centrally located, people from many other states often participate." Some of the people she has met on the walk have become good friends.

Store and restaurant owners along the route are very much aware of the walk. Once when Teresa and a friend were walking through the Haymarket district, they stopped at the Bleu Moon for a break. "A jazz band was playing," Teresa remembers, "and the owner offered free soft drinks or coffee with a meal purchased by anyone on the walk. We enjoyed ourselves so much that it was more than an hour before we left."

Most of all Teresa likes watching the families have fun together on the walk. "There is no hurry to finish," she says, "so the walk can be done at a child's pace. I know of one family who makes a whole day outing of the walk. They pack a picnic lunch and take as much time as they want to stop and visit the museum and art galleries along the way. When it's lunchtime, they stop at one of the city parks and eat before continuing on their way."

EASTERN NEBRASKA

Wilderness Park Hiking Trail (66)

Directions: The trail is located on the southwest edge of Lincoln. From I-80, take the downtown exit, Ninth Street south, to Van Dorn Blvd. west to First Street.

Best Season: Spring and fall; but summer and winter are also good times to walk this trail, and there are opportunities for cross-country skiing in winter.

Length: 13 miles; you can walk all or part of the trail.

Degree of Difficulty: Easy. The terrain is level, and the trail is well-maintained year-round.

Highlights: A chance to experience a wilderness which is in close proximity to the city.

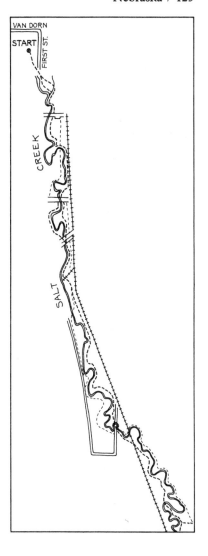

"Wilderness Park offers an unforgettable experience for any hiking enthusiast," says Terry Genrich, who nominated this walk. The jogger will find a jogging exercise trail along the walk, the history buff will find numerous features of interest, including remnants of structures which housed Chautauquas in the late 1800s and early 1900s, and the nature lover will find an area of beauty, tranquility, and peace.

Following Salt Creek, the wood-chipped trail winds through the 1,455-acre linear park, which is mostly comprised of the flood-plain vegetation typical to the area along the waterways of eastern Nebraska. "The habitat is mostly mixed hardwood deciduous forest," Terry Genrich explains, "with several stands of burr oak and hackberry along the trail."

The path leads through heavily wooded areas, meadows, and creek beds and over a number of bridges, including an arched and a suspension bridge and several footbridges. For the observant walker, a host of treasures may be discovered along the trail: an abundance of wildflowers, fallen trees with cavities where animals can hide or make their homes, and lots of wildlife—raccoon, opossum, cottontail, white-tailed deer, and fox. There is also a wide variety of birds and, according to Terry, "It's not unusual to flush a covey of quail or even spot an owl or hawk."

There are several good walking tours of the city of Lincoln, Nebraska's capital, and you certainly don't want to miss a visit to the capitol building, which occupies four square blocks between K and H and 14th and 16th streets. The complex design was voted the fourth architectural wonder of the world in a nationwide poll of architects and is an Art Deco masterpiece. Within its dome are six huge mosaics depicting themes of Nebraska history. From the outside, you get a view of the dome and the giant statue of *The Sower*, carrying a bag of seed on his shoulder. There is also a statue of *Lincoln* near the capitol's west entrance. This was made by Daniel Chester French, who, among other things, created the statue of *Lincoln* in the Lincoln Memorial in Washington, D.C. For more information about tours of the capitol and other walking tours of Lincoln, stop in at The Tourist Information Center, located on the corner of O and Ninth streets. It's open every day from June to mid-September.

EASTERN NEBRASKA

Winsome Woods Walk (67)

Directions: The walk is located in the Schramm Park State Recreation Area, 25 miles southwest of Omaha. From I-80, take exit 432 to Route 31 south. Pick up a self-guided brochure inside the Ak-Sar-Ben Aquarium at the main entrance to the park.

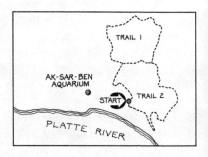

Best Season: September through mid-October.

Length: "It's possible to run through in about two hours," say nominators Jan Moritz and Dick Zlab, but they strongly suggest making a day of it. The hiking distance is 3 miles round-trip.

Degree of Difficulty: Moderately difficult. There are some steep trails. Stay on the path to avoid an unwanted encounter with poison ivy.

Highlights: Fish ponds shared by ducks and swans, perfect river views, the sounds of birds, the fragrant smell of wildflowers, sunlight radiating through thick foliage—all contribute to the wonderful serenity of this walk which the nominators describe as a place where "nature encompasses and holds every living thing in a time warp, if only for a few precious moments."

Two major hiking trails (called "Winsome Woods Walk" by our nominators), each 1½ miles in length, loop back to back through the natural woodlands of Schramm Park. The first trail begins a little way from the Ak-Sar-Ben Aquarium. Before or after your walk, plan to spend some time in this exceptional aquarium which features native fish, a terrarium, and regular showings of films and slide presentations. The aquarium is closed on Tuesdays throughout the year, otherwise the hours are from 10 a.m. to 5 p.m. on weekdays, 10 a.m. to 7 p.m. on Saturdays and Sundays from May 15 through September 15, and from 10 a.m. to 4:30 p.m. daily the rest of the year.

As you leave the aquarium (through the east doors), follow the service road to the Trailhead. Before actually beginning the walk, you'll pass several small fish ponds. "If you're lucky," say nominators Jan Moritz and Dick Zlab, "the lily pads will be in full pink-and-white bloom, reaching for the very large blue sky." The Trailhead is just to the left of the first pond.

Along the trail itself, each of the plants and trees is carefully marked, and numbers correspond to the informative brochure of the area. We learn, for example, that the Indians used the fruit and leaves of the red cedar to make cough syrup and that their bows and arrows and ceremonial pipes were made from the green ash. The leaves of the prickly ash, a shrub, were chewed as a remedy for toothache, and the Omaha used the fruit of this same shrub as a perfume.

The first loop of the well-marked trail consists of evergreen and hardwood trees, shrubs, wild prairie flowers, vines, and fruit bushes. The terrain is hilly, steep enough in some places for railroad-tie steps and strategically placed rest areas. A meditation shelter, donated by an anonymous walker, provides a perfect place to relax and take pictures. Its pyramid shape was designed for the visitor to gain maximum appreciation of the surrounding beauty.

The second trail loop is more primitive: The pathways are narrower and there's a stream to cross with steep banks. From several clearings, there's a beautiful view of the sandbarred Platte River winding in the valley below. Those who walk quietly are likely to see a wide variety of wildlife darting in and around the trail: rabbits, squirrels, coyotes, minks, foxes, deer, raccoons, opossums, beavers, muskrats, and skunks. Birds, too, provide a feast for the careful eye, and a list of birds that may be spotted is available at the aquarium.

Nominators Jan and Dick so enjoyed their "Winsome Woods Walk" that they urge you not to cut it short. "You'll miss more than you can ever imagine," they say. Their enthusiasm for this special place is best described in their own words: "The descriptions and feelings were conveyed easily by one of us through sight. For the other, different senses were every bit as salient as vision. The leaves sounded like falling snow on a very still winter morning. The laughter of the children and the friendly greetings of fellow hikers were filled with happiness and a radiating warmth. The texture of the leaves turning colors from green to yellow and from orange to red felt different at every stage. There is virtually no limit (except that placed by time) to the experiences that can be gleaned from this walk, and they are experiences open to everyone."

EASTERN NEBRASKA

Historic Fort Omaha (68)

Directions: Exit I-680 at 30th Street in Omaha and drive south 2½ miles to the main gate of the fort at Fort Street. The walk begins at the General Crook House at the corner of North and West roads.

Best Season: April through October.

Length: 1.3 miles; an hour to an hour and a half.

Degree of Difficulty: Moderate. Note that there is one short hill to climb.

Highlights: This walk through the historic fort that housed the headquarters of the Department of the Platte includes the commander's home and the site of the famous 1879 hearing of Standing Bear.

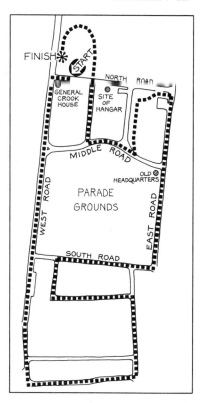

This walk through historic Fort Omaha was nominated by Barbara Lokke. It begins at the General Crook House with a stroll through the magnificent Victorian Gardens which are in bloom most of the year. General Crook, a Civil War hero, was one of the Army's most effective Indian fighters. From 1875 to 1882 he was the Commander of the Department of the Platte whose duty was to protect settlers from Indian attack. Despite his reputation as an enemy of the Indian, General Crook defended Indian rights in the trial of Ponca Indian Chief Standing Bear. Crook enlisted the help of Omaha attorneys, and in the final court decision in this landmark case, it was stated that an Indian was a "person" within the meaning of the law. Barbara says that the sad story of the peaceful Indian farmer Standing Bear was recently filmed and will air on educational TV channels. The filming took place at the fort and in the General Crook House, as well as in other parts of Nebraska.

From Crook House, this walk leads to the parade grounds and past the animal buildings, which are about 100 years old. The route passes by General Crook's headquarters and the Administration Building which was home to a World War I Balloon School; you'll see the site of the huge hangar that once housed a giant dirigible. Today the New Education Building stands in its place.

Barbara Lokke grew up less than a mile from the fort and this area is very special to her. She loves the large old trees that make the

82½-acre fort almost like an unexpected park in the middle of the city, and she likes to experience the history of the place. She says that when she shows people around the fort, she tries to make the past come alive and to link it with the present. "I want visitors to hear the bugle's call across Nebraska's treeless plains," she says. "I hope they will see the balloons in Omaha's skies, just as thousands of people saw them in the World War I era."

The walk ends back at the General Crook House where you can tour the inside from 10 a.m. to 4 p.m. Monday through Friday, and 1 to 4 p.m. on Sundays. The house was built in 1878 and has been perfectly restored with antiques from the period.

Across the street from the fort's main entrance gate is the famous Mister C's Restaurant—well known for its year-round Christmas lights and its excellent food. Barbara tells us that during the Christmas holidays of 1971, one of the waitresses at the restaurant whose husband was stationed at Fort Omaha asked Mr. C (Caniglia) to leave the Christmas decorations up until her husband returned from overseas duty in January. The year was half over before he actually returned home, but the lights were waiting for him, and they are still burning.

WEST CENTRAL NEBRASKA

Saddle Rock Trail (69)

Directions: The trail is located in Scotts Bluff National Monument, on the western edge of Nebraska's panhandle, 3 miles west of Gering, and 5 miles southwest of the town of Scottsbluff. Take I-80 to Kimball, then go north on Highway 71 to Gering and west on Highway 92 to the Scotts Bluff National Monument Visitor Center.

Best Season: Fall or spring.

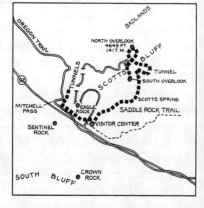

Length: 1.6 miles; about an hour to the summit and forty-five minutes to descend.

Degree of Difficulty: Moderate. There's a steady incline, but the pathway is in good condition. Nominator LuVerne Knoedler cautions to be on the lookout for rattlesnakes in the fall.

Highlights: A beautiful panorama of the North Platte River Valley and the Oregon Trail from the summit.

This trail begins at the Visitor Center in Scotts Bluff National Monument, passes through a tunnel and joins a half-mile-long trail at the summit where there are spectacular views of the North Platte River Valley, Chimney Rock, and Laramie Peak from the north overlook and of the Oregon Trail from the south overlook.

Nominator LuVerne Knoedler especially likes this trail because it "combines a nature walk with a hill walk amidst beautiful scenery." It's also chock-full of history, and LuVerne suggests you "walk in the ruts of the Oregon Trail wagon trains" once you've come down from the summit.

It is perhaps difficult for today's visitor to appreciate the significance of landmarks such as Chimney Rock and Scotts Bluff to the early pioneers. But a look at their journals conveys some of the thrill they must have felt upon reaching these strange formations. They could see Chimney Rock for two days before they actually got to it, and we know it was important to them for it is the most frequently mentioned of all landmarks in pioneer diaries.

Chimney Rock, Scotts Bluff, and the other "high spots" seen by the pioneers are remnants of a high plain formed by clay, volcanic ash, and sandstone swept down by winds and floods from the Rocky Mountains some 25 million years ago. Capped with hard sandstone, these remnants have survived the erosion that caused the disappearance of the rest of the "high plains" which were once hundreds of feet higher than the present Great Plains.

Today you can ride a wagon train or go on horseback to the base of Chimney Rock where you'll meet fur traders and Indians, see the Pony Express, and dine on food cooked over the campfire. To really get into the spirit, plan to bring the whole family to the "Oregon Trail Days" celebration in Gering. For three days in July, the clock is turned back, and everyone's a pioneer, joining in parades, barbecues, dancing, and contests.

Scotts Bluff National Monument includes 3,000 acres of prairie habitat and Scotts Bluff itself, which rises 800 feet above the North Platte River. Visit the museum at the Visitor Center and enjoy the paintings and photographs of pioneer artist William H. Jackson.

As you leave the Scotts Bluff National Monument, head south on Route 71 and stop at the Wildcat Hills State Game Refuge. Here, amid Ponderosa Pines, you'll share space with bison, elk, and deer. There are a few bobcats and wild turkeys as well.

North Dakota

EASTERN NORTH DAKOTA

A Look around Downtown Fargo (70)

Directions: Fargo is located at the intersection of I-29 and I-94. Take Main Avenue to Broadway and pick up a self-guided brochure at the Visitors Bureau, 701 Main Avenue, where the walk begins.

Best Season: Year-round, weather permitting.

Length: Allow at least half a day.

Degree of Difficulty: Easy.

Highlights: Becky Purdy, who sent us this walk, says it "provides a look at historic buildings representing the growth of a region."

In the year 1892, Fargo, North Dakota, was an important city of over 8,000 people. It had experienced fantastic growth since it was first laid out in 1871, especially in 1878, when fifty new buildings went up in as many days. There seemed no end to the building boom in this bustling town. Then, on June 7, 1893, the town's dreams literally "went up in smoke." Ninety percent of the city was lost within the span of a few hours when a fire, which started on Front Street, quickly spread and wiped out downtown Fargo. This walk recaptures some of the fighting determination residents must have felt as architects went to work rebuilding the city.

The predominant architectural styles of postfire Fargo are Neoclassical and "Richardsonian" Romanesque. Both tend toward massive structures of stone, with the neoclassical buildings sporting enormous columned porticoes, brick pilasters, metal cornices, and raised brick parapets while the Richardsonian Romanesques were less ornate with mainly stone trim.

First stop on the tour is the Northern Pacific Railway Depot at 701 Main Avenue. This is an excellent example of the Richardsonian Romanesque style. The architect was Cass Gilbert, who also designed the Minnesota State Capitol. The Powers Hotel at 400 Broadway is considered one of the finest examples of the Neoclassical style.

Two buildings along the tour survived the fire and reflect the popularity of Victorian Gothic before the fire. The Luger Furniture Store at 716 Main Avenue was built in 1882, and the Masonic Block at 9–11 Eighth Street South, was built in 1884.

There are 53 buildings on this tour and one statue, the Rollo Statue, at Fifth Avenue North and Broadway. It commemorates Gange Rolf, the founder of Rouen, France, and the first duke of Normandy. The inscription on the plaque reads: "For World Peace Normans United."

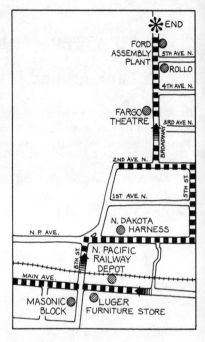

Two buildings of particular interest are the North Dakota Harness Company Building at 627–29 N.P. Avenue and the Fargo Theater at 213–16 Broadway. The Harness Company Building was built in 1905 for a company that supplied horse collars and harnesses to the farmers of Red River Valley prior to the use of tractors. The Fargo Theater, built in 1926, was the best of its era and still has its original marquee. Step inside for a fascinating view of the building's Art Moderne interior.

The walk ends at the Ford Assembly Plant at 505–511 Broadway. Built in 1914, it is one of several similarly designed Ford plants in the United States. A spur line of the Great Northern Railroad runs right inside the building where cars were assembled and then loaded onto the train.

CENTRAL NORTH DAKOTA

Downtown Bismarck (71)

Directions: The walk begins at the old Northern Pacific Depot on Main Avenue.

Best Season: Year-round.

Length: Allow about three to four hours.

Degree of Difficulty: Easy.

Highlights: Historical trivia abound in this tour of North Dakota's capital.

Located on the hills overlooking the Missouri River, Bismarck began flourishing in the 1870s when the Northern Pacific Railroad reached the Bismarck steamboat port. At that time, Yankton was the state capital, although a number of "boom towns" were challenging Yankton for this privilege. None of these growing towns succeeded until June 2, 1883, when, after much political maneuvering (including a meeting on board a train at five in the morning), Bismarck became the new capital.

Nominator Candice Gartner loves to visit the old railroad depot where this walk begins. "It's been renovated within the past six to eight years," she says, "and seven coats of paint were removed before the beautiful mosaic tiles you see now were uncovered. There's a Mexican restaurant in the depot now; the kitchen used to be the baggage room, and the bar was once the ticket office." But the depot has not been entirely abandoned by the railroad. Every day at noon the Burlington Northern comes through.

One of the most amusing stories about the depot concerns the Kewpie doll. "Inside the depot," Candice says, "stuck in the stucco, are eleven china Kewpie dolls. Apparently, when the building was being constructed, a Mexican man who was doing the stuccowork received word that his wife back in Mexico had had their eleventh child. In honor of the birth, he went out and bought eleven Kewpie dolls in a local Bismarck store and imbedded them into the wall."

Another historical fact is commemorated by a marker at the spot where the telegraph office stood. It was from this office that the defeat of General George Armstrong Custer at the hands of the Sioux at Little Bighorn in 1876 was broadcast to the world.

Other sights on the walk through Bismarck include St. Mary's Catholic Church, the oldest church in Bismarck, and the McKenzie Hotel, which was built in 1910 and almost torn down in the 1970s. Today it is home to the Peacock Alley Bar and Grill, where you can view pictures of the hotel at its peak and examine all sorts of memorabilia including old hotel bills and menus. The rooms of the hotel serve today as housing for the elderly.

Candice also recommends a visit inside the Burleigh County Courthouse, which contains murals and plaques depicting North Dakota history, and a trip to the recently restored former Governor's Mansion, which is located on the outer edge of the downtown area.

WESTERN NORTH DAKOTA

Jones Creek Trail (72)

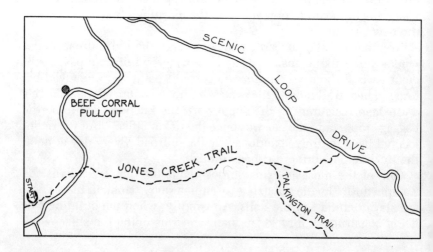

Directions: The trail is located in the south unit of Theodore Roosevelt National Park. Exit Highway 94 at Medora, and follow signs to Park Headquarters.

Best Season: June through September.

Length: 3.7 miles, but plan to spend as much time as you can in this incredibly unique area of the United States.

Degree of Difficulty: Moderate.

Highlights: The craterlike landscape of the Badlands is baffling as well as awe-inspiring, especially to the first-time visitor.

Nominator Bruce Kaye feels that the 3.7-mile Jones Creek Trail, which follows a creek and runs through the heart of the Badlands, is one of the most representative of the area. Some say this region got its name from the settlers who crossed the prairie with relative ease only to be met by the harsh, unfriendly buttes and ravines that characterize this part of North Dakota. Others say the term *badlands* came from French-Canadian trappers, and still others believe it originated with the Sioux. Whatever its origins, it's not difficult to understand the sentiment behind it, although "bad" in this case is also "beautiful" in a startling, impressive sort of way.

The sculptured forms were created as erosion from wind and water molded the soft strata of previously deposited sediment that had come from the Rocky Mountain region. These eroded formations were capped by layers of hard sandstone. "The contrasting colors of the various exposed rock layers are striking," Bruce says, "and not unlike the colors one sees in Death Valley." Interestingly, the Badlands are not nearly as barren as they may look at first glance. There is a variety of wildlife, including many species of birds, and a great number of wildflowers and shrubs. Even bison and elk, which had become extinct in the area, have been reintroduced to the park and are doing fine.

Here in the Badlands the bison once roamed in abundance and the little town of Medora became a center for hunting enthusiasts from the east, including Theodore Roosevelt, who actually became a part owner of a cattle ranch in the area. Medora was founded in the 1880s by a Frenchman known as the Marquis de Mores. He named the town for his wife and built a twenty-seven-room chateau to provide aristocratic living right in the middle of the Badlands. You can visit this impressive home which is open to the public for tours.

The region made a lasting impression on Theodore Roosevelt, who once said, "I never would have been President if it had not been for my experiences in North Dakota," and the Badlands helped to shape his firm commitment to conservation. After his death in 1919, many people in North Dakota urged the creation of a park in the Badlands in memory of Roosevelt. Few listened at the time, but when the lackadaisical and sometimes nonexistent interest in conservation led to the Dust Bowl disasters of the 1930s, much of the barren land was taken over by the federal government and restored. Part of this restoration became the Theodore Roosevelt National Park.

Ohio

SOUTHEASTERN OHIO

Lakeshore Trail (73)

Directions: The walk is located in the Ironton Ranger District of Wayne National Forest, 7 miles north of Ironton on Route 93. It begins at the Vesuvius Backpack Trailhead at the Lake Vesuvius boat dock.

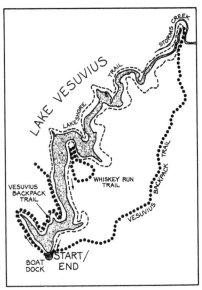

Best Season: Spring, winter, and fall.

Length: An 8-mile loop.

Degree of Difficulty: Easy.

Highlights: Lake views, beaver dams, wildflowers, and a creek crossing are of special interest on this leisurely walk, which you may want to extend into an overnight adventure.

According to Deck Hunter, who has done a lot of volunteer work for the hiking trails of Ohio and who has written a pocket guide of several trails, the Lakeshore Trail is an especially good one for beginning hikers or for anyone who wants a relaxed, overnight experience in the forest. The scenery is beautiful in spring and fall, but nominator Lionel Lemery likes it best in winter, especially when there is a light snow covering.

Follow the Vesuvius Backpack Trail for about a mile. It will break off at that point, and you'll take the Lakeshore Trail along the lake to a swimming area. Picnic tables behind the beach house make this a good place to stop and eat, if the time is right. After about another

139

mile, watch for trillium along the hillside (if it's springtime), and a little farther on you'll notice pointed tree stumps—signs that beaver have been busy cutting the trees. Continue along the path to the large boulder, which provides an excellent resting place with beautiful views of the lake.

Once past the three-mile marker, watch for a sharp turn in the trail to the left, and head downhill to Storms Creek. If you have planned to spend the night, walk along the wider Jeep Trail to the pine forests, where campfires are permitted unless there is a fire hazard due to dry weather. Registration is not required to camp here, but you should check ahead of time for specific information and to make sure there is no fire hazard. Call the Ironton district ranger at (614) 532-3223.

In the morning, cross the stream and continue along the Lakeshore Trail which joins the Vesuvius Backpack Trail again for a short distance and then intersects with the Whiskey Run Trail. Here you can take a little half-mile side excursion to a cavelike overhang. Whiskey Run Trail passes by an old whiskey still and abandoned charcoal pits and then loops back to the Lakeshore Trail a little farther south along the lake.

Follow the trail to another picnic area in front of an old historic open-hearth furnace.

SOUTHEASTERN OHIO

Ohio View Trail (74)

Directions: The trail is located within Wayne National Forest, northeast of Marietta. Follow the sign on State Route 7 at the northern edge of Beavertown for the Southern Trailhead. The Northern Trailhead is along the south side of State Route 260, approximately 3 miles west of New Matamoras.

Best Season: Year-round.

Length: 7 miles.

Degree of Difficulty: Moderately difficult. There is a long steep climb uphill at the southern end, and some short climbs throughout, as the trail traverses draws in the slopes of the hills.

Highlights: "On this trail," says nominator Marilyn Ortt, "you can see the whole Ohio River Valley much as it must have been 200 years ago."

Climbing up from the Ohio River, this spectacular trail meanders through forests of various sizes and composition and in and out of coves on up to the ridges where there is a beautiful vista of the Ohio River, with tugboats often in sight. Marilyn Ortt, who nominated the walk, tells us that you can see Long Reach from the top. It was so named by George Washington because it is the longest straight portion of the river.

"For most of walk you are under a deciduous canopy of trees," says Marilyn, "with occasional vistas of the Ohio River, its broad floodplain, and the hills of West Virginia." The northern half is not so close to the river, but you can enjoy a wealth of wildflowers and a variety of habitats. Be sure to keep an eye out for the occasional foundation stone or piece of barbed wire, testimony to the hill farms of long ago, but now almost completely engulfed by the growth of tree trunks.

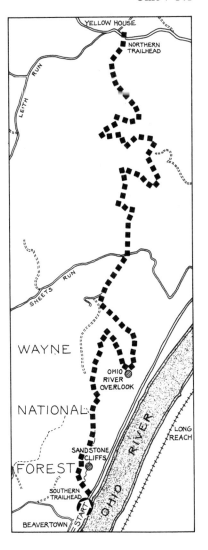

This is the bicentennial of Marietta, Ohio, and the whole Northwest Territory, and while development has certainly changed the landscape, here on top of the ridge there are unspoiled views of the river, of the scattered farms below, as well as some industry. As a closing affirmation to the beauty of the place, Marilyn says, "I have recommended this trail to numerous people from out of town. They are all impressed."

For more information, contact: Little Muskingum Station, RR No.1, Marietta, OH 45750; (614) 373-9055.

NORTH CENTRAL OHIO

A Walking Tour of Oberlin (75)

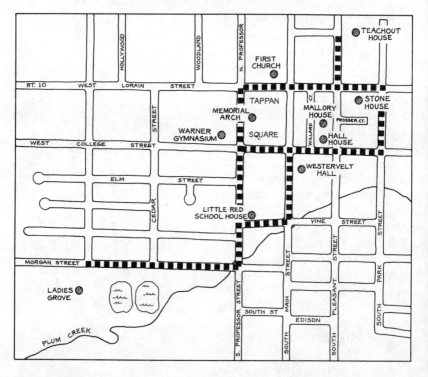

Directions: From Toledo, head east on Route 90 (the Ohio Turnpike); from Cleveland, head west. Exit at Route 58. Oberlin is just south of the turnpike at the intersection of Routes 58 and 10. This walk begins in the center of town at Tappan Square.

Best Season: Spring and fall, but the walk can be enjoyed year-round.

Length: About 3.1 miles; allow two or three hours.

Degree of Difficulty: Easy.

Highlights: Spectacular architecture amid picturesque English-style landscaping in a culturally sophisticated college town.

Nominator Bob Yun calls this walk "a cultural feast for the mind and eye." This is an apt description because the community of Oberlin reflects a truly exemplary blending of the diversity and culture found in a college community with the warm tradition of midwestern small-town charm. Bob tells us the town was once described as "a twentieth-century college campus surrounded by a nineteenth-century Ohio village."

The walk begins at Tappan Square in the center of the community. A self-guided tour brochure is available from the Friends of Oberlin, Inc., located in Monroe House, 73½ South Professor Street, Oberlin, or at the Oberlin College Inn on Tappan Square. The beautifully landscaped square is proof of the town's diversity. It contains an arch constructed in memory of twelve Oberlin missionaries killed in China's Boxer Rebellion, a newly dedicated bandstand, modeled after an Indian festival cart, and an "historic elm" tree planted near the site of Oberlin's first log cabin.

Surrounding Tappan Square are the buildings of the Oberlin College campus and a myriad of "century" homes restored to their original charm. The architecture is so varied that it has been said that "you can stand at the plaque in the center of Tappan Square, turn on your toes through a 360-degree arc and almost box the compass of the architectural history of the western world."

The walk takes you past Mallory House at 58 E. College Street, one of the town's first dwellings. Built in 1838, it was remodeled in 1932 in accordance with its Federal style by Oberlin architect William Durand. A few homes away, at 64 E. College, is Hall House. A fine example of Italianate architecture, it was the home of Charles Martin Hall, an Oberlin college alumnus who founded Alcoa Aluminum and at whose bequest Tappan Square was constructed. Westervelt Hall on South Main Street exemplifies Victorian Gothic architecture, the Stone House on North Park is a rare example of a sandstone block house, Teachout House on North Pleasant is the oldest surviving example of the French mansard style, the First Church on the corner of Main and Lorain streets is an example of Greek Revival, and Warner Gymnasium (on the aptly named Professor Street) is "Richardsonian" Romanesque. Bob Yun says that "Finney Chapel, Peters Hall, Carnegie Library, Wilder Hall, and the old Music Conservatory are testaments to the vision of an age when local sandstone was used to create edifices of lasting impression and utility. The more contemporary design of the new Music Conservatory and Hall Auditorium provides striking contrast, yet does not distract from the elegance of the older neighbors.

Many of these buildings are not just there to be viewed on the exterior. Visitors are encouraged to tour the College Art Museum, listen to a concert, or attend a theater performance at Finney Chapel. There are plenty of places to shop and eat in nearby downtown Oberlin, which has been recently renovated to echo its cobblestoned, gaslit-streets past. The past is felt, too, in a visit to such places as the Little Red School House, built in 1837 as the first school for children in Oberlin and Ladies Grove, south of Morgan Street. To describe Ladies Grove, the tour brochure quotes the college rules of 1859: "'Young ladies who do not reside with their parents are not allowed to walk in the fields or woods excepting the grove assigned for this purpose.' [Here in Ladies Grove]...Antoinette Brown and other women students convened their own debating society because they were not allowed to take part in public debating."

Throughout this walk, the manicured lawns and gardens are reminiscent of the English countryside. All in all it's hard to imagine a more fulfilling walk than this all-encompassing tour of Oberlin, which is, indeed, a "cultural feast."

CENTRAL OHIO

Lancaster Historic District (76)

Directions: Lancaster is located in South Central Ohio, 19 miles southeast of I-70. From Columbus, take I-70 to Route 33 south. Follow 33 to

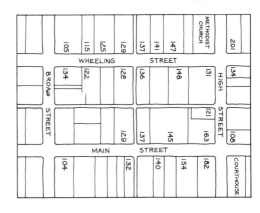

Lancaster. The historic district is two blocks east of Route 33.

Best Season: Spring, summer, fall.

Length: Less than half a mile; allow at least thirty minutes.

Degree of Difficulty: Easy, but the streets do have slight inclines.

Highlights: An outstanding collection of early nineteenth century architecture set in an area of historic interest.

The town of Lancaster, Ohio, has a unique origin. In 1796, the Congress decided a roadway was needed through the sparsely settled Northwest Territory, and it commissioned the Zane brothers—Ebenezer, Jonathan, and Noah—to construct it. The roadway was to extend from Wheeling, West Virginia, to Limestone, Kentucky, to make it easier and more appealing for people to go west and stay there. In return for their efforts, the Zanes were to receive three square miles of land each along three rivers in Ohio.

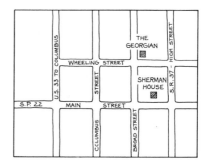

The brothers completed their roadway, known as Zane's Trace, and in 1800, they laid out a town along the Hockhocking, one of the rivers they had received in payment for the job. The town was called Lancaster, and by 1801 it looked pretty much the way it does today. The Zanes began selling lots in their new town, and by the 1820s 2,000 people called the place home. The town flourished and so did its population. Huge homes were constructed by the newly wealthy Lancastrians, symbols of affluence which can be enjoyed by visitors to the town today as one of the finest collections of nineteenth century architecture to be found anywhere in the country.

This walk, nominated by Mary Luttrell, covers what is known as Square 13, which is listed in the *National Register of Historic Places*. Square 13 is one of the original blocks of Lancaster laid out by the Zane brothers. Most of the homes are privately owned, but Mary says the owners are very proud of them, and there's a good chance to "meet and greet" the property owners.

Two of the homes are owned and operated by the Fairfield Heritage Association and are open to the public Tuesday through Sunday, from 1 to 4 p.m. (the homes are closed in January and February). The Georgian, at 105 East Wheeling Street, was built in 1833 by Daniel Sifford for Samuel MacCracken, a prominent businessman and fund-raiser for the Ohio Canal System. It boasts an imposing portico with five fluted Ionic columns, each one encasing a whole tree trunk.

Sherman House, located at 137 East Main Street, contains a replica of General Sherman's field tent with Civil War exhibits, as well as treasured items belonging to the Sherman family, including the family-album quilt and two examples of Mary Hoyt Sherman's silk-on-silk needlework.

Following your walk around Lancaster, plan to spend an hour or two in the beautiful Hocking Hills State Park. Take Route 33 south to Route 180 and follow signs to the park, which is divided into six uniquely charming units, dominated by the Black Hand, a sandstone formation with deep gorges and dramatic cliff overhangs. It is named for the black hand painted on a sandstone cliff east of Columbus. It is believed that Indians drew the hand to indicate a source of flintstone. Wildflowers and wildlife are abundant in Hocking Hills, as well as spectacular waterfalls, caves and rock shelters. Winding trails throughout allow the walker to experience the wilderness up close.

CENTRAL OHIO

Forest Rose Cemetery Walk (77)

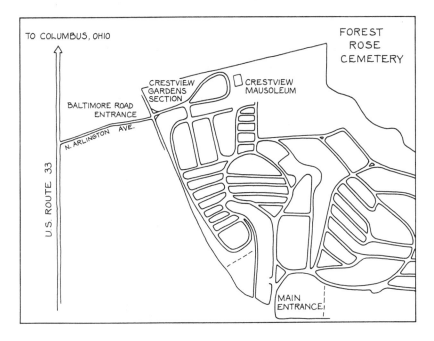

Directions: From Route 33 in Lancaster, take Arlington Avenue to the cemetery entrance, one-half mile from Route 33.

Best Season: Year round.

Length: Varies. Nancy Goodman and Patty Peery, who nominated this walk, average about 6.5 miles.

Degree of Difficulty: Easy to difficult. The walk can be used as an exercise workout: warming up on level ground, then climbing to higher ground for more strenuous exercise.

Highlights: An opportunity to get great exercise in a peaceful, beautiful setting: the walk also provides a history lesson on the area.

We could not resist including this walk, which was submitted to us as "the most unusual walk in the midwest" by Nancy Goodman and Patty Peery of Lancaster; we think it would make a unique change of pace after your walk through Lancaster's historic district (see page 144).

Forest Rose was originally two cemeteries: German Lutheran and English Lutheran. Around 1882 it was combined into one 65-acre cemetery. According to the nominators, it is beautiful at any time of year, with a variety of trees and shrubs and gorgeous flowering plants in spring and summer. From the higher elevations, there are superb views of the whole city of Lancaster, with particularly good vistas of Mt. Pleasant. It's a wonderful place to walk, the nominators say, especially at sunrise or sunset. Its quiet, tranquil setting, with no traffic and no traffic lights or city noises, makes it perfect.

Nancy and Patty walk as partners, sharing stimulating conversation and observing the surrounding graves and mausoleums. "Many of the founders and early settlers of Lancaster are buried in this cemetery," Nancy says, "and the epitaphs provide insight into their lives."

Their walks in Forest Rose have earned Nancy and Patty the title of "Forest Rose Cemetery sentries," and they take it very seriously. Sometimes they will notice something that doesn't seem quite right, and they will bring it to the attention of the caretaker. "Once we noticed that a person had been buried under the wrong name," Patty remembers, "and once the inscribed date of death was in the future."

These walks have stimulated an interest in taking walks in other cemeteries, and Nancy and Patty feel that they learn new things every time. "We have come to be able to recognize good stonework," Patty says, "and we have gained an appreciation for older tombstones and their symbols." Most of all, the walks are a place to enjoy good conversation and to ponder some of the deeper questions of life. "If we ever had any morbid feelings about being in a graveyard," Patty declares, "they no longer exist."

CENTRAL OHIO

The Dawes Arboretum: Maple, Holly, and Oak Trails (78)

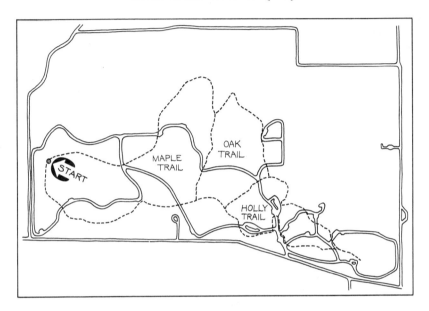

Directions: From Columbus, take I-70 to exit 132 and drive north for 3 miles on Route 13. The Dawes Arboretum is 5 miles south of Newark.

Best Season: May and October.

Length: The Maple Trail is 0.7 mile; the Holly Trail is 1.2 miles; the Oak Trail is 2.4 miles. There's lots to see here, so allow at least half a day.

Degree of Difficulty: Easy to moderate; gently rolling terrain.

Highlights: A Japanese garden, facsimile prairie, holly collections, cypress swamp, and fern and wildflower gardens are just some of the delights of this walk.

This is an unguided walking tour of three trails which loop out from the Visitors Center and return there. Each trail is clearly marked by posts and is further defined by close mowing or a covering of wood chips. An excellent interpretive brochure, available for a returnable deposit, gives interpretive texts for each stop along the trails. Information is provided in three areas: nature, history, and horticulture, and each is separated into two age levels: young children and older children and adults. In this way, everyone who walks the trails can learn about the plant and animal habitats and about the geology and history of the place on a somewhat individualized level. Emphasis is placed on the interdependence of the plants and animals and ourselves. This was one of the reasons Alan Cook nominated the walk. "The trails give a sense of the relationship of people," he says, "past, present, and future to plants (native and exotic) and animals."

Along all three of the trails, you'll find deciduous woods, fern and wildflower gardens, cypress swamp, and giant white pine. On the Holly and Oak trails there's an evergreen forest, a Japanese garden, a facsimile prairie with a prairie garden, an early-settlers' cemetery, and an old log cabin. The arboretum also includes a fascinating holly collection, rare and dwarf wood plants, a high overlook with superb views, persimmon trees, Dawes Lake, and the world's longest (2,840 feet) hedge of letters, which spells out "Dawes Arboretum."

NORTHEASTERN OHIO

McKinley Monument, Canton (79)

Directions: Take I-77 to the Fulton Road exit. Follow signs.

Best Season: Fall or spring is best, but "anytime is great," says Pat Garrett, who sent us this walk.

Length: The Cemetery Walk is about 2 miles.

Degree of Difficulty: Easy (you can bypass the steps up the monument).

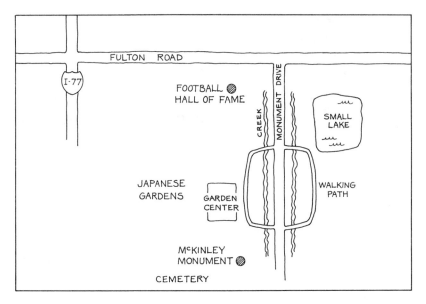

Highlights: Historic monument, an eighteenth-century cemetery, beautifully landscaped areas, a small creek, and a lake are all part of a walk through this area.

William McKinley, the twenty-fifth president of the United States, was born in Niles, Ohio, and grew up in Poland, Ohio. But he practiced law in Canton, and it is here that he is remembered. A memorial, 97 feet high and 75 feet in diameter at the base, was dedicated to McKinley's memory in 1907. Inside is a statue of the president delivering his address at the Pan-American Exposition in Buffalo, New York, on September 5, 1901. It was, of course, his last speech. The following day, as McKinley stood in a reception line shaking hands with the public, he was shot. He died a week later. The statue built in his honor by Charles Henry Niehaus stands 9½ feet high and is secured to a 13-foot pedestal.

There are several walks in the McKinley Monument area. Nominator Pat Garrett prefers the Cemetery Walk, directly behind the monument, because it's peaceful and beautiful and never crowded. A nature walk nearby leads alongside a creek where you can watch the ducks. It's especially wonderful in the spring when the parent ducks have their babies in tow. Pat tells us this walk is lit until 11 p.m. in the summer, and she says it's very romantic after dark when the light reflects through the trees. Another enjoyable area where Pat likes to relax is the Canton Garden Center which has a woodsy Japanese garden setting.

If you're a sports fan, you know that Canton is famous for the Pro Football Hall of Fame. Be sure to stop in for a visit after your walk in the McKinley Monument area.

NORTHEASTERN OHIO

Gorge Trail, Youngstown (80)

Directions: This walk is located in Mill Creek Park. Take I-680 to Youngstown, Glenwood exit. Drive south on Glenwood to Route 62, then west on 62 to the Mill. Watch for signs.

Best Season: Year-round. Each season has its own unique beauty.

Length: About 2 miles; allow three-quarters of an hour to an hour and a half.

Degree of Difficulty: Moderate. There are some stairs and a gently sloping terrain.

Highlights: A beautiful waterfall, stream, and numerous scenic views.

Nestled in the heart of Mill Creek Park, the east and west sides of the Gorge Trail take the walker on a breathtakingly beautiful walk which includes a boardwalk designed to help protect the delicate ecosystem from foot traffic and to allow easier access to an area that is largely mud, washouts, and slippery trails. The boardwalk covers about 350 yards and follows the ups and downs of the gorge past massive stone outcroppings, including Umbrella Rock, which is thought to have provided shelter from the elements to the Indians long ago.

There is a bridge at either end of the trail to allow people to cross over Mill Creek. The Silver Bridge, at the northern end, was built in

1895 as a suspension bridge, and it still retains its lovely nineteenth-century charm. The southern-end bridge is for pedestrians and affords a magnificent view of the gorge below. For family fun and safe adventure, nominator Thomas Bresko suggests crossing the stream here on the "stepping stones."

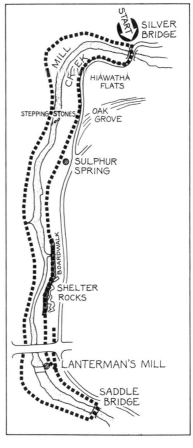

Mill Creek Park was established in 1891, and there are several sites along the trail that reflect another era. Lanterman's Mill, for example, on the southern end of the trail, is considered one of the finest restored gristmills in Ohio. Powered completely by water, it operates today just as it did when it was first constructed in 1845. Hiawatha Flats is an area reportedly used as an Indian campsite. It was named after the play *Hiawatha* which was performed there by Indians in 1916.

The walker's nose will be the first to recognize Sulphur Spring, created in the late 1800s by testing done for coal mines. At that time it was thought the waters had medicinal benefits, especially for kidney ailments and rheumatism, but this later proved to be untrue. Today the spring provides welcome refreshment to walkers. Don't worry about the sulfurlike smell; the waters are tested semiannually to be sure they are safe.

The gorge was formed over millions of years as the trickling waters of Mill Creek cut a pathway through the sandstone. The Gorge Trail is bordered on one side by the stream and on the other by stone. For most of the way, the walker rubs shoulders with the massive rocks, 60 to 100 feet high. The trail is also lined with hemlock, beech, maple, and oak trees. Thomas Bresko says that Christmas fern, Solomon's seal, and skunk cabbage are abundant and challenges the walker to find out why they are so named. "Touch the touch-me-nots," he urges. "Identify a bird by its song. Or spot the ever-present chipmunk, its pouchlike cheeks filled with seeds." And watch for the huge carp lurking below in the dazzling pools of water. "Having visited most urban parks throughout Ohio," says Bresko, "I find this 2-mile jewel of a trail one of the most rewarding."

NORTHEASTERN OHIO

City-Sewer Trunk Line Hike, Akron (81)

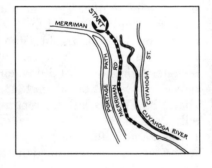

Directions: Take Route 8 to West Market Street in Akron. Drive to the intersection of Merriman Road and Portage Path. Park at any of the several small shopping areas.

Best Season: Year-round, except when snowy or icy.

Length: About 5 miles round-trip; allow at least two hours.

Degree of Difficulty: Moderate; the walk can be slippery when wet.

Highlights: Scenic views from a unique perspective.

Nominated by Omagene Smith, this walk along the main trunk line of Akron's sewer system is, indeed, unique. The trunk line is a masonry and cement conduit, 10 feet in diameter, through which all of Akron's sewage is moved to a very modern disposal plant farther down the valley. It was built in the mid-1920s and was laid in the bed of a section of the old Ohio Erie Canal which passed through Akron and the Cuyahoga Valley. All of this section is aboveground and is of sufficient size to walk on top of it comfortably.

The walk begins on Merriman Road, a few yards south of the intersection of Merriman and Portage Path. Cross the railroad tracks to get on the sewer line and head south through both shaded and open areas with views of the meandering Cuyahoga River. You'll pass the Valley View Golf Course, where in the summer you can kibitz with the golfers from your lofty perch on the trunk line.

After about 2 miles, the elevation of the ground rises and the sewer consequently disappears underground. You can turn around at this point and retrace your steps, or, if you want a longer hike, an old service road continues to the Memorial Parkway where a series of left turns will take you across the little Cuyahoga River, then across Uhler Street to Cuyahoga Street. Proceeding north on Cuyahoga Street, turn left into a dirt driveway just past the City Correctional Facility. This driveway goes back to an old abandoned bridge where the river can be recrossed, and by following any of the several unmarked trails, you can again locate the sewer line for a stroll back to the start.

If you're hungry, Omagene suggests you try one of the many "choice spots" close by: Bill Crocker's Bar & Grill, Hibachi Japan, E. J. Hamads, Carnaby Street Inn, or the Wine Merchant (noted for its imported wines).

The nearby Weathervane Community Playhouse, located on Weathervane Lane, might be a good way to end your day. For nearly fifty years the playhouse has provided first-class live entertainment, and many actors and actresses who started at the Weathervane have gone on to stardom in the movies, on television, or on Broadway.

WEST CENTRAL OHIO

A Walk through the Country Common (82)

Directions: This walk begins in Glen Helen, a 1,000-acre nature preserve which belongs to Antioch University, in Yellow Springs. From I-70, take exit 52A to U.S. 68 south. Continue for 10 miles to Yellow Springs. Turn left on Corry Street (the first traffic light) and go one-third mile to the Glen Helen parking lot on the left. The preserve is open to the public only during daylight hours. The walk begins at the Glen Helen Trailside Museum on Corry Street.

Best Season: Year-round, but nominator Ralph Ramey particularly likes the last week of April and the first week of May and the middle two weeks of October.

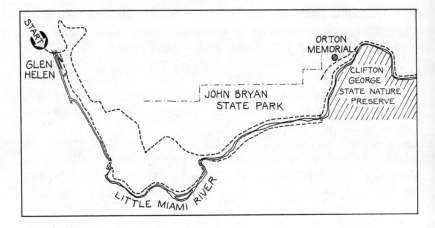

Length: 12 miles; about four and a half to five and a half hours.

Degree of Difficulty: Moderate; there are a few rocky spots along the trail.

Highlights: A woodland trail that passes an old gristmill and follows the scenic Little Miami River to the spectacular Clifton Gorge.

"Country Common," says Ralph Ramey, nominator of this walk, "is the name given to the collective of parks, preserves, camps, and open-space easements between the villages of Yellow Springs and Clifton." The walk he recommends combines trails through the Glen Helen Nature Preserve, John Bryan State Park, and Clifton Gorge State Nature Preserve.

Near the Glen Helen Trailside Museum is the Raptor Center, where sick or injured birds of prey are cared for until they can be returned to the wild. Stop in before or after your walk; you can usually see a turkey vulture or two, several hawks, owls, and perhaps even an American bald eagle.

Follow the trail past the Swinging Bridge and on into John Bryan State Park, a 500-acre park on the Little Miami River. A narrow trail leads along the rim of Clifton Gorge and affords a breathtaking view of the river far below. The gorge is a result of the steady flow of the river eroding the rocks.

The power of the Little Miami River provided a source of energy for saw- and gristmills, and industries flourished here in the early

1800s. At that time, the Cincinnati-Pittsburgh stagecoach followed the river through the gorge and stopped at Yellow Springs, where people would take "water treatments" from the supposedly healthful spring waters. Long before the white settlers came to these springs, the Indians, too, had considered these waters "health-giving," and many of their trails passed by it. According to Clarence Leuba in his *Guide to Historical Spots in Glen Helen*, a small but very informative guidebook of the area, one of these Indian trails, the Bullskin Trace, led to Detroit and was used to take prisoners, including Daniel Boone and Simon Kenton, to that city to collect the ransom offered for them by the British. The Shawnee Indians used this trace in the other direction to get to their hunting grounds in Kentucky.

SOUTHWESTERN OHIO

The Riverwalk, Cincinnati (83)

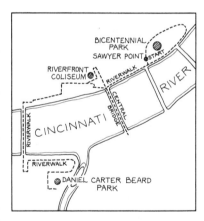

Directions: You can pick up this walk from Bicentennial Commons at Sawyer Point on Cincinnati's riverfront.

Best Season: Spring, summer, autumn.

Length: 4 miles; allow at least a half day; there's lots to do and see.

Degree of Difficulty: Easy.

Highlights: Sawyer Point, a riverfront recreational area, a geologic history of Cincinnati, and floating restaurants are just a few of the highlights on this unique, brandnew walk.

In 1788 and 1799, three settlements were founded on the Ohio River at the site of present-day Cincinnati. One of them, Losantiville, (meaning the "town opposite the mouth of the Licking River") was renamed Cincinnati in 1790 by Arthur St. Clair, governor of the Northwest Territory. By 1810, Cincinnati had become the largest city in Ohio. Today it is a dynamic, energetic city, proud of its accomplishments and dedicated to being a true "people's city." Nowhere is Cincinnati's enthusiasm more evident than in its bicentennial Riverwalk Project. The walk, according to nominator Sara Backman, was dedicated in October 1988 and encircles the Ohio River from Northern Kentucky to Cincinnati, connecting the riverfronts of Cincinnati with those of Covington and Newport, Kentucky.

Along its 4-mile route, the walk includes thirty-five historical stations. Seven of them are life-sized "participatory" statues which one artist has called the "finest collection of realism in the twentieth-century." They are referred to as "participatory" because they are not statues on pedestals, but right on the ground, posed in everyday positions, where people can go right up to them, touch them, sit down with them, etc. "For example," Sara says, "one statue is of James Bradley, the first black man to be admitted to a college in Ohio. Bradley sits on a park bench with an open book on his knees. People can share the bench with him."

Surrounding the Riverwalk is Bicentennial Commons, a $14-million riverfront recreational area with tennis courts, skating rink, amphitheater, and more. In addition, on the Cincinnati side of the walk, there's a Geologic Timeline, depicting the geologic history of the Ohio Valley, spanning 450 million years; on the Kentucky side, you'll be able to enjoy any of several floating restaurants aboard one of the romantic, old-fashioned riverboats.

Oklahoma

CENTRAL OKLAHOMA
Oklahoma City Walk (84)

Directions: Oklahoma City is located at the juncture of I-35 and I-40 in the middle of Oklahoma. The walk begins at ArtsPlace, 20 West Main Street.

Best Season: Year-round, but April is a particularly good time as there is an annual Festival of the Arts.

Length: 1 to 1½ miles; allow about an hour and a half.

Degree of Difficulty: Easy.

Highlights: This walk through the skyways and tunnels of Oklahoma City is both fun and educational.

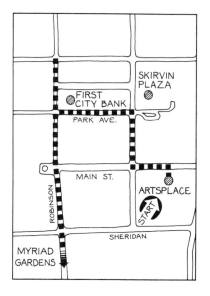

Oklahoma City grew up in the middle of an oil field, and, as if to prove it, a working oil well stands on the front lawn of the state capitol. Of course, no one knew about the oil (which wasn't discovered until 1928) when Oklahoma City was incorporated in 1890. From nothing more than barren prairie, the city now encompasses some 620 square miles, its modern skyline rising impressively on the horizon, testimony to a commitment to development and industrial expansion. But the city is not all industry and manufacturing. Oklahoma has more shoreline (artificially made) than the whole Atlantic coast, and numerous lakes in Oklahoma City provide fishing, swimming, and hiking.

This walk of the downtown area originated about fifteen years ago as part of a city project to introduce school children to the various art and cultural experiences the city offers. The tour changes every year and can be customized to suit the walker's particular interest.

159

There is a charge for the tour which is conducted by trained docents, and reservations are necessary. For more information, call (405) 232-1787.

The walk begins at ArtsPlace, a gallery which is part of the Oklahoma Arts Center. The building itself is believed to be the oldest in Oklahoma City, dating to 1906, one year before Oklahoma became a state. From here you'll walk over skyways and through tunnels (nominator Elizabeth Hahn says the tunnels are filled with "wonderful sixties graphics and murals by high school kids") as you explore the history, culture, and architecture of the city. These skyways and tunnels are so popular with the citizens of Oklahoma City that you see few people in the streets. "Visitors always think it's a holiday here," Elizabeth says.

Near ArtsPlace is the old Skirvin Plaza Hotel, built in 1910 and a good example of the elegant old-style hotels of that period, complete with chandeliers in the elevators. Several presidents have stayed at the Skirvin and even today it merits a four-star *Mobil Guide* rating. From April 1 to October 31, docents also lead walking tours of downtown Oklahoma City from the Skirvin every Friday at 10:30 a.m.

On North Robinson, you'll pass a contemporary office building with a sculpture by Alexander Lieberman in front. Step inside to see the magnificent silk-screen art panels in the lobby. At Robinson and Park, the First City Bank building provides a prime example of the Art Deco style, with aluminum swans, aluminum trim, and thirteen kinds of marble. Farther down Robinson at Myriad Gardens, you'll have a chance to enjoy some of the lakes that add so much charm to Oklahoma City. This beautifully landscaped retreat includes a botanical garden, fountains, and the "Crystal Bridge," a glass cylinder in the center filled with tropical plants.

NORTHEASTERN OKLAHOMA

Tulsa Art Deco Walk (85)

Directions: The walk is located in the central downtown district of Tulsa. Begin at the Tulsa Union Depot, 3 South Boston Avenue.

Best Season: Spring, early summer, and autumn.

Length: From 1 to 2½ miles; about one to two hours.

Degree of Difficulty: Easy, just obey the traffic lights

Highlights: A variety of new and restored architecture offers contrasting views of eras and values.

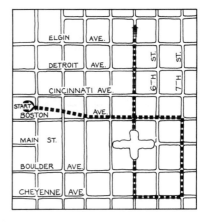

Along with Miami Beach and New York City, Tulsa, Oklahoma, is considered one of the premier Art Deco cities in the United States. Nothing more than a tiny village when it was incorporated in 1898, Tulsa began exploding after oil was discovered there in 1901. This growth continued and coincided with the emerging Art Deco design style that became extremely popular during the 1920s and 1930s. Basking in the monetary sunlight of gushing oil, a million dollars a month was spent in Tulsa's downtown area.

This walk is centered around Tulsa's Main Mall where the magnificent buildings, with their sleek, imaginative forms express the "modernism" of the times and represent a distinct contrast to the steel and glass architecture of the newer Tulsa buildings. But, according to nominator Nancy Miller, "The terra cotta Art Deco empire of the twenties and thirties blends remarkably well with our modern architecture. There was so much terra cotta used in construction during this period that Tulsa became known as 'Terra Cotta City.'"

Tulsa's history is intricately tied to the nation's move westward, for this was Indian Territory, home to the Osage, Creek, and Cherokee, and, in fact, Tulsa's skyscrapers stand on the site of an Indian village. In 1889, the United States government opened the area to white settlers offering nearly 2 million acres of Oklahoma land to anyone who staked a claim. A pistol shot began the "run," and those who jumped the gun and got there first were called "sooners," thus, Oklahoma's nickname as the "Sooner State." Prior to statehood in 1907, Oklahoma was divided into two territories—the Indian Territory and the Oklahoma Territory.

A visit to the Gilcrease Museum will give you an opportunity to learn more about Tulsa's history. In addition to Indian exhibits, there are paintings and sculpture by artists of the Old West, including Frederick Remington, George Catlin, and Charles Russell.

NORTHEASTERN OKLAHOMA

Tsa-La-Gi, Cherokee Heritage Center (86)

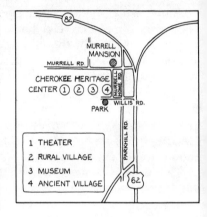

Directions: Tsa-La-Gi is located between I-40 and I-44, 60 miles east of Tulsa and 3 miles south of Tahlequah, along Highways 51, 62, 82, and 10. Take the Willis Road exit and follow signs to the Cherokee Heritage Village.

Best Season: May through August.

Length: The ancient village is under 3 acres in area, but it is located on a 44-acre site, and it would not be difficult to spend all day in this fascinating place.

Degree of Difficulty: Easy.

Highlights: A wealth of history and a chance to walk around a replica of a sixteenth-century Indian village.

"Tahlequah is the headquarters of the Cherokee Nation of Oklahoma, which covers fourteen counties in northeastern Oklahoma," says nominator Linda Vann. The village of Tsa-La-Gi, 3 miles south of Tahlequah, is a reconstructed sixteenth-century Cherokee settlement. Trained guides explain the lifestyle in the village, and visitors can watch baskets being weaved, pottery taking shape from mounds of natural clay, and arrowheads and blowguns being shaped from native stone and cane. You can also see villagers playing a game of stickball and watch a demonstration of a stomp dance which was part of a religious ceremony.

Tahlequah is important to Cherokee history for it was here that the Cherokee settled after they were forced to move from their homes in the east. From June 11 through August 20, the drama of this exodus which is historically known as "The Trail of Tears" is portrayed in an outdoor amphitheater in Tsa-La-Gi. It is a moving story and not a pleasant one, for the Cherokee were an advanced agricultural nation well before the Pilgrims landed at Plymouth Rock. But the white settlers spelled disaster for the Cherokee; half the tribe died from smallpox in the 1750s. Then, when gold was discovered on their lands, a fraudulent treaty forced them to move west. In 1838, they started on their "Trail of Tears." Thousands died before they could reach Tahlequah. Today some 45,000 Cherokee live in Oklahoma.

There is also a rural village, or crossroads community, on the grounds which depicts Cherokee life at the turn of the century. This is open year-round, but it comes to life as another "living museum" only in the summer. A school, a general store which sells items similar to those of the time period, and a cabin are part of this village. Visitors can observe demonstrations in the making of lye soap and candles, watch a game of horseshoe pitching, and participate in a school lesson in the Cherokee language.

South Dakota

WESTERN SOUTH DAKOTA

Deadwood's Boot Hill (87)

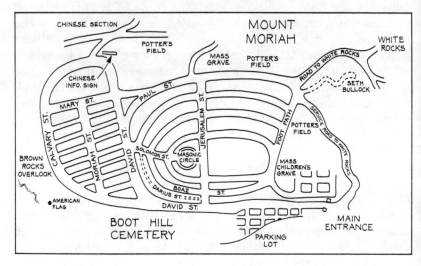

Directions: From Rapid City, take I-90 west to U.S. Highway 14A southwest. Drive about 13 miles to Deadwood.

Best Season: Fall.

Length: About forty-five minutes.

Degree of Difficulty: Easy.

Highlights: Historic cemetery overlooking Deadwood Gulch and the Black Hills.

A part of the Mount Moriah Cemetery, Deadwood's Boot Hill transports the walker back to the exciting days of the wild, wild west. Although you cannot personally meet the famous and infamous former residents of Deadwood (except maybe in spirit), it is not hard to imagine these hardy souls exerting their influence on the frontier
164

town. Boot Hill boasts the markers of Wild Bill Hickok; Calamity Jane;
Potato Creek Johnny, a prospector who took out the largest gold nug-
get ever found in the northern Black Hills; Preacher Henry Weston
Smith; and Seth Bullock, the first sheriff of Lawrence County and a
lifelong friend of Theodore Roosevelt. As nominator Connie Heier
says: "It's all here—on the mountain overlooking Deadwood—the
town's history, her famous and her unknowns, her preachers and her
patrons. And it's fascinating. Even the view is terrific, especially in
late September when the trees in Deadwood Gulch turn the golden
colors of fall."

Romance, adventure, and tragedy are all part of your tour of Boot
Hill. For example, Wild Bill Hickok, gambler and gunslinger, and
fellow gambler Calamity Jane are buried just a short distance from
each other—at Calamity's request. The many miners buried on the
hill remind us that "adventure" was the siren song urging many of
them west to places like Deadwood with promises of gold, gold, and
more gold. And there was more than enough tragedy. A mass children's grave attests to the horrors of disease; this particular epidemic
swept through the Gulch in the late 1800s. Another mass burial section holds the graves of eleven miners who died in a boarding-house
fire in 1883.

There's also a Chinese section in the cemetery, and Connie says it
"literally hangs on the mountainside as if the dead were awaiting
removal to their homeland, as was the custom of the day."

For a look at a working gold mine, drive southwest on Route 14 a
short distance to the town of Lead. A lead (pronounced "leed") is a
lode, or vein, of ore, and this town got its name from the famous
Homestake Lode that was discovered here. Today more gold comes
from the Homestake Mine than any gold mine in the Western Hemi-
sphere.

EASTERN SOUTH DAKOTA

Three Trails around Big Stone Lake (88)

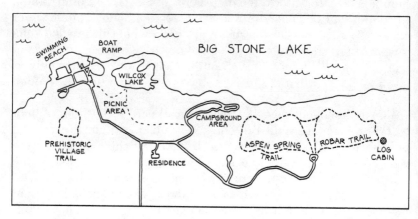

Directions: Big Stone Lake is located in Hartford Beach State Park. From I-29, take exit 213 east to Wilmot and drive about 25 miles. Watch for signs to the park.

Best Season: Summer.

Length: The Robar Trail is ¾ mile; Aspen Spring Trail is ½ mile, and the Prehistoric Village Trail is ¼ mile. Allow about an hour and a quarter for all three.

Degree of Difficulty: Moderate; the Prehistoric Village Trail is slightly hilly.

Highlights: A chance to view archaeological sites in a scenic place with lots of wildlife.

Robar Trail

The big stone which marks the beginning of the Robar Trail, named for pioneer trader Solomon Robar, also marks a number of graves. Four of the graves are children's, two of them the children of Solomon Robar, and there is also the grave of Robar's wife—all silent reminders of just how difficult life was for the early pioneers.

The rocks are also representative of the many rocks along the shores of the lake and up on the bluffs. In fact, the Indians gave the lake two names. They called the lower part Lake of the Big Stones, in honor of the rocks; the upper part they called Bent Lake, because of its bow shape.

Big Stone Lake is 38 miles long and covers more than 22,000 acres. The abundance of valuable wildlife in the area—buffalo, otter, mink, and beaver—made this place a particular favorite of the early trappers and traders, and four different countries—France, Spain, England, and the United States—have called it theirs over the years. The original trail to the Robar Trading Post is south of the current trail, and on the old road you can still see the deep ruts cut by hundreds of wagon wheels.

As you follow the trail, you'll come to Solomon Robar's Trading Post where there are also two log buildings which were used as cellars for the storage of food and furs. Solomon Robar was a Frenchman, and his wife was an Indian, half Chippewa and half Sioux. She acted as a midwife in the area, and her knowledge of herbal medicine helped alleviate the pain and sickness of many of her neighbors.

Aspen Spring Trail

This trail affords a quiet, restful walk through a hardwood forest filled with babbling springs and creeks. You may spot any number of animals, including beaver, mink, raccoon, muskrat, weasel, fox, badger, and rabbit. Buffalo and otter no longer exist here.

Prehistoric Village Trail

This short, but steep, trail leads to the top of a bluff where you'll have an excellent view of Big Stone Lake and of prehistoric burial mounds across the valley. Indians used to gather around these mounds for ceremonial dances and powwows.

The archaeological digs in this area have shown that prehistoric peoples lived here 10,000 to 15,000 years ago. One of the sites is believed to be a fortified prehistoric village on the bluffs.

EASTERN SOUTH DAKOTA

In and around Brookings (89)

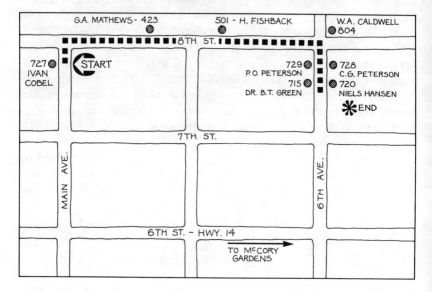

Directions: From Sioux Falls, take I-19 to exit 132. Drive west about 1½ miles to Main Avenue in Brookings. The walk begins at the Ivan Cobel home at 727 Main Avenue.

Best Season: Summer and early fall.

Length: About half an hour without stopping.

Degree of Difficulty: Easy.

Highlights: Eight distinctly different historic homes, a visit to a garden research center, and a trip to the world of *Little House on the Prairie* are all part of this tour in and around Brookings.

Brookings is known as the agricultural capital of South Dakota and the surrounding prosperous farms give credence to the title. But this walk, nominated by Carol Bain, begins in the town itself and leads past eight homes listed on the *National Register of Historic Places*. Each of these homes is privately owned, so the visitor cannot go inside, but their varied exteriors provide a wonderful opportunity to compare architectural styles.

First on the tour is the Ivan Cobel House at 727 Main Avenue, on the corner of Eighth Street. Built in 1920, it exemplifies the Prairie style, an elaboration, really, of the basic bungalow. Turn right on Eighth to No. 423. This example of Queen Anne architecture was constructed in 1896 for G. A. Mathews, an early resident of Brookings who, as an active member of the town's government (he was mayor several times) required that trees be planted in the city.

At 501 Eighth Street, you'll find a Neoclassical home that was built in 1902 for Horace Fishback, who, with his uncle, began the first banking institution in Brookings. It was nothing more than a counter in the general store he owned, with a safe somewhere in the back. A few years later, in 1882, Fishback and his father organized the first national bank in the county.

Another example of Neoclassical architecture stands at the corner of Eighth Street and Sixth Avenue. This house, built in 1902 for W. A. Caldwell, a president of Farmer's National Bank, was converted to apartments in 1920 and renovated in 1986.

Crossing Eighth, you'll see at 728 Sixth Avenue the C. G. Peterson House, another Queen Anne–style structure, and across the street at No. 729 is the P. O. Peterson House, a Victorian "eclectic," which at one time sported a wraparound porch. Down the street at No. 715 is a gambrel-roofed South Dakota clapboard, the former home of Dr. B. T. Green, who practiced medicine in Brookings from 1904 to 1931.

The last house on the tour, at 720 Sixth, was built in 1897 by P. J. Bergeim, a contractor who built this home for himself but sold it a year later to Niels Hansen, a professor of horticulture and forestry at South Dakota State College. It is a fitting end to a walk through the historic section of Brookings because the next stop is the McCory Gardens on Route 14 at the east end of town. Here you can wander through trial gardens established by South Dakota State University to determine a species' ability to adapt to the South Dakota climate.

From the gardens, drive west on Route 14 to De Smet, which is the town depicted by Laura Ingalls Wilder in her *Little House on the Prairie* books. Many of the sites she described are open to the public.

EASTERN SOUTH DAKOTA

Woodland Trail (90)

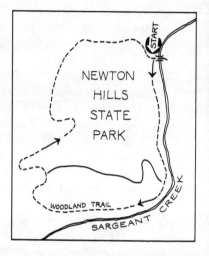

Directions: The trail is located in Newton Hills State Park, 30 miles south of Sioux Falls and 6 miles south of Canton. Pick up a self-guided trail brochure at the Trailhead.

Best Season: Spring and fall.

Length: Approximately 1 mile; allow at least an hour.

Degree of Difficulty: Moderate; there is varying terrain with some steep slopes.

Highlights: Diversity of flora and fauna; Indian and early pioneer folklore; unusual geologic and glacial formations.

"The Woodland Trail is a photographer's paradise!" exclaims nominator Marty DeWitt. "From the first sprouting shoot of the snow trillium in spring to the blinding snowstorm in winter, one can view firsthand the many faces of Newton Hills. Birds, flowers, and wildlife abound and the colorful fall foliage provides many photo opportunities."

The trail, which has been designated as a National Recreation Trail by the U.S. Department of the Interior, begins at the bridge over Sargeant Creek, named for Tom Sargeant, an early settler. Long before the trails and roads of the park were built, the area of Newton Hills, part of the geologically fascinating Coteau des Prairies ("hills of the prairie"), was so secluded that, according to legend, it was used as a hideout by horse thieves and as a burying ground for stolen treasure. Today the legend lives in the name given to the ravine you'll view as you hike along the trail: Horse Thief Canyon.

Artifacts and burial mounds in the area indicate that prior to the arrival of the white settlers, Woodland Indians occupied the region from about 300 B.C. to around 900 A.D., followed by the Great Oasis Indian Culture, and eventually the Sioux. One of the Sioux legends tells of an Indian chief who was captured by an enemy tribe. Condemned to death in the "quick mud" of the Nehimi Springs, the captured chief cursed his enemies, predicting that white men would drive them away and turn Newton Hills into a barren desert. He was only half right.

As you follow the Woodland Trail, be sure to consult the excellent trail guide which corresponds to numbered stations along the walk. The guide identifies the various trees and shrubs as well as the many unique prairie and woodland wildflowers, and points out such oddities as "puffballs," which can be found in the thickets along the trail. Indians used the powdery spores of the puffballs on cuts to stop the bleeding.

The guide also reminds you to look for the homes of birds and animals in the trees along the trail. Raccoons, for example, often live in the large tree cavities, while the round holes you see in the tops of dead trees are the doorways to woodpecker dwellings. More than 200 species of birds visit the park throughout the year, and in addition, deer, marmots, rabbits, red and gray foxes, opossums, squirrels, and wild turkeys live there.

If your trip takes you to Sioux Falls, plan a visit to Sherman Park at the western edge of the city. There's a zoo there, a 1,600-year-old Indian mound, and a memorial to the battleship *USS South Dakota*. A short drive northeast from Sioux Falls on Route 11 will take you to the town of Garretson and Devil's Gulch, a narrow gap in the towering pink quartzite cliffs above Split Rock Creek where it is said Jesse James hid out after an unsuccessful bank robbery.

EASTERN SOUTH DAKOTA

Trail of the Spirits (91)

Directions: The trail is located in Sica Hollow State Park in the northeastern corner of South Dakota. Take I-29 to exit 232 at Sisseton. Drive 4 miles west, through Sisseton, and then 7 miles north and 6 miles west to the park. Follow signs.

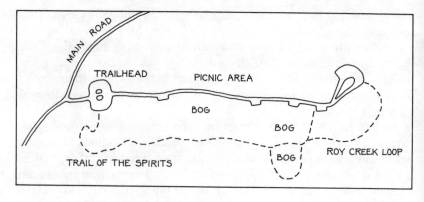

Best Season: Spring for wildflowers; fall for magnificent foliage; winter for cross-country skiing.

Length: ½ mile; about three-quarters of an hour (but plan on staying much longer).

Degree of Difficulty: Easy.

Highlights: A walk into the mysterious land of *sica* (pronounced "SHE-cha"), which means in the language of the Sioux "bad" or "evil" spirits, and a chance to see magnificent long-range views and plants and animals found nowhere else in South Dakota.

A number of reasons led the Santee or East River Sioux Indians to name this place *sica*, that is, bad or evil. First of all, there were the hills, known as the *Coteau des Prairies* ("hills of the prairie") to the French fur traders. What were they doing on this otherwise flat plain? In fact, the hills, which rise in some places to more than 2,000 feet above sea level, were formed during the Wisconsin glaciation. Nominator Dave Daberkow says that when the glacier receded, the Coteau was left standing as a high land.

And then there were the bogs created by the many gurgling springs in Sica Hollow. Indian legend, inspired perhaps by an actual sighting of a child or animal falling into one of the bogs, has it that a terrible monster lived underground, just waiting to reach up and grab anyone who came close. As if proving the legend true, the bogs are often stained red. The Indians could not know that this is due to the iron content of the water.

And then there was that ghostlike aura at dusk. What could it be, if not the spirits gathering? In fact, the mysterious glow is fox fire, or "swamp gas," a product of methane gas, created from decaying vegetation. But even you or I walking the hollow today would probably not know that.

And what were those groans from the bog in early spring, if not the cries of underground spirits? Even today no one is sure what the strange noise is. It is believed that air becomes trapped in the bog during winter. As the seasons change and it becomes warmer, it is theorized that the air is gradually released, making sounds such as those made when you blow over the top of a bottle.

Trail of the Spirits is a wonderful opportunity for the walker to explore a fascinating land of legends, to enjoy the plant and wildlife, and to imagine what it must have been like to roam these hills 200 years ago. The trail begins at the footbridge over Roy Creek, named for the Roy family who came to the area in the early 1840s and stayed there as the first white settlers.

The self-guided brochure is one of the best we've come across. Numbered stations along the trail correspond to numbered explanations in the brochure so that the walker can easily identify plants, trees, and shrubs and learn all sorts of fascinating things about them. More than twenty-five rare species can be found in Sica Hollow; wild ginger, for example, the Dakota skipper butterfly, and the gray tree frog. And Sica Hollow is the westernmost home of the sugar maple. You'll pass by the largest one in the state.

Dave Daberkow suggests that when you have finished your walk along the Trail of Spirits, you spend some time exploring the rest of Sica Hollow. There are numerous trails in the 860-acre park which take the walker from the lower, more humid areas all the way up to the top of the Coteau. Perhaps you will agree with the Indians that the higher elevations are more peaceful and friendly. Many tribes ascended the highest hills to pray or fast or seek communion with *Wakantanka*, the "great spirit."

EASTERN SOUTH DAKOTA

Sand Lake Wildlife Refuge (92)

Directions: The refuge is 27 miles northeast of Aberdeen. From Aberdeen, take U.S. 12 east to County Road 16. Drive 20 miles north, through Columbia, to the entrance. From Sioux Falls or Watertown, take I-29 north to exit 232. Go west on Highway 10 about 70 miles, then south 5 miles to the Visitor Center.

Best Season: Spring and fall. The refuge is open from early April to late October.

Length: There are miles of roads leading through the refuge. You can walk all of them or plan a combination walk/drive.

Degree of Difficulty: Easy.

Highlights: A wide variety of bird and animal life in a setting of marshes, woodlands, croplands, and prairie grasslands.

The 21,451 acres of the Sand Lake Refuge lie in the rich, rolling lowlands of the James River Valley and include four distinct habitats: marsh and open water, woodlands, grasslands, and croplands. Each one offers its own rewards to the visitor, especially the visitor on foot, who can explore the area intimately and share it with the birds and animals who live there.

Large shallow lakes, formed by the slow-moving James River, are the heart of the refuge and afford an opportunity to see an unparalleled variety of waterfowl: geese, pelicans, ducks, herons, hawks, grebes, sandpipers, gulls, and terns are just some of the more than 260 different species of birds that have been recorded since the refuge was established in 1935.

The woodland habitat is not natural to the region. Trees were planted as windbreaks and now serve as home to squirrels and mourning doves and other species which previously were uncommon or unknown around Sand Lake. The grasslands hold numerous surprises for the walker who may think, at first, that nothing is there but the tall grasses. Underneath, however, are tunnels built by mice. The hawks soaring overhead know how to find them as do the red fox and skunks who search for food amid the grasses.

The croplands were also introduced into the area to provide food and cover for the birds and animals. These crops include corn and grain as well as "weed patches," which are a mixture of wheat grass, alfalfa, and sweet clover planted in strategic locations to improve nesting conditions for ducks and other wildlife.

Carol Bain, who nominated this walk, suggests you begin your visit to Sand Lake with a stop at headquarters for information and a climb up a 108-foot tower for a "bird's-eye view" of the refuge. To get an idea of the significance of this place, remember that with the arrival of the white settlers in 1887 and their subsequent use of the land for farming and grazing, most of the wildlife in the area had been eliminated by the 1930s. Thanks to the refuge, today it is much closer to what it was prior to the intrusion of people and efforts continue to preserve and restore it. For example, a captive flock of 300 giant Canada geese are maintained, and several thousand have been released into the wild so that some day this species, near extinction in 1962, will be restored to its former range in the Dakotas.

Wisconsin

SOUTHEASTERN WISCONSIN

Parnell Tower Area Loop, Ice Age Trail (93)

Directions: The trail is located in the northern unit of Kettle Moraine State Forest. From Milwaukee, take Highway 57 north to Route 23 west. The Trailhead is just south of the town of Greenbush.

Best Season: Year-round.

Length: 4-mile loop.

Degree of Difficulty: Moderate.

Highlights: An opportunity to view glacial topography and to witness firsthand the enormous power of the ice age glaciers.

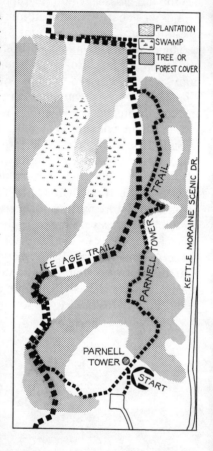

The Ice Age Trail was created as a complement to the Ice Age National Scientific Reserve in an effort to provide an opportunity to study the unique landscape formed by the glaciers that once covered much of Canada and the northern United States. The trail totals 400 miles, and there are plans to complete an additional 600.

Nominator Bill Moorman likes the Parnell Tower Trail best because it provides the most dramatic and most concentrated examples of the effects of the glaciers. Much of Wisconsin's landscape is

176

a result of these glaciers, and as you walk along the trail, you will be able to witness their power. The names of these glacial effects sound as though they're from a dictionary found on a distant planet. *Eskers*, for example, are winding ridges of sand and gravel that were formed by a river that flowed under the ice. And *kames*, Bill says, are "gumdrop-shaped hills caused by debris falling through a hole in the ice." They are perfectly formed because the hole acted as a funnel, channeling the debris as if it were sand. And there are *kettles*, or depressions, in which bodies of melted blocks of ice collected in areas from 100 feet across to 20 acres; and, nearby, *drumlins* are a series of elongated hills which are the result of ice-transported debris left behind when the ice melted. For more information on the effects of the Ice Age, be sure to visit the Ice Age Interpretive Center located in the forest, a quarter mile south of Dundee on State Highway 67.

This extremely scenic trail is well marked and passes through hardwood forests of red oak, basswood, sugar maple, shagbark hickory, white oak, and red maple.

SOUTHEASTERN WISCONSIN

Milwaukee's Third Ward (94)

Directions: This tour of the Third Ward begins at 330 N. Water Street.

Best Season: Year-round.

Length: Allow about half a day.

Degree of Difficulty: Easy.

Highlights: Buildings from the past receive "new life" in this fascinating historic district.

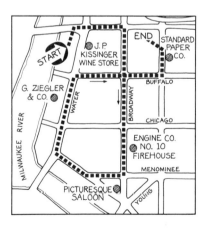

Contrary to popular belief, Milwaukee's leading industry is not beer but electric power, and there are so many other industries in the city that Milwaukee has been dubbed "the machine shop of America." At the juncture of three rivers—the Milwaukee, the Menominee, and the Kinnickinnic—Indians gathered at the site of present-day Milwaukee long before the white people came, and they called it *millioki* or "the gathering place by the waters." From the time Solomon Juneau founded a trading post on the riverbank in 1818, the community continued to grow and was eventually incorporated as a city in 1846.

This walk through Milwaukee's Third Ward was nominated by Tracey Carson. Located near the harbor, the river, and the railroad, this district became a thriving wholesale and manufacturing center. In the beginning, raw products such as fish, lumber, hide, and grain were shipped east. Then, in 1856, when the railroad linking Milwaukee with the Mississippi River was completed, the goods also began traveling west.

Everything went along smoothly until 1892 when a fire broke out on Water Street and virtually destroyed the entire district. Nineteen-hundred people, most of them Irish laborers, were left homeless. But reconstruction began immediately, and the district soon rose to even greater economic importance, only to be devastated once more by the depression and World War II. The warehousing activity of the Third Ward never again regained its former significance, but during the late 1970s, the Third Ward began attracting investors interested in adaptive reuse of the buildings. In 1984, ten blocks of the area were accepted on the *National Register of Historic Places*.

This walk, which begins at the Victorian-style J. P. Kissinger wine store, will take you past some of the most interesting and important buildings in the ten-block Historic Third Ward district. At 176 N. Broadway, for example, you'll see the Engine Co. No. 10 Firehouse. Built in 1893 on the site of the only firehouse in Milwaukee to be destroyed by fire, the building is a beautiful example of the Queen Anne style. A survivor of the fire, the picturesque saloon at 226 E. Erie Street is in marked contrast to the firehouse. Built between 1888 and 1892, it is in the "flat iron," or wedge-shape, style that was typical of many of the tiny homes that once stood in the Third Ward.

There's another survivor of the fire at 223 N. Water Street. This building was constructed in 1890 for George Ziegler & Co., candy makers, and the first firm in all Wisconsin to make marshmallows.

The walk ends, appropriately enough, at a warehouse. The commercial-style building at 316 N. Milwaukee Street was built in 1914 for Standard Paper Co., and has an entrance canopy trimmed with green art glass.

For more information about the Historic Third Ward and a free *Historic Third Ward Walking Tour* brochure, write or stop in at the Historic Third Ward Association Office, 203 North Broadway Street, Milwaukee, WI 53202, or call (414) 273-1173.

SOUTHEASTERN WISCONSIN

Lake Michigan Harbor Walk, Racine (95)

Directions: The walk is located in downtown Racine, about a half hour from Milwaukee and an hour and a half from Chicago. Take I-94 to exit 333 (Highway 20) and take Highway 20 east to Racine. The walk begins at the Visitors' Center at 345 Main Street.

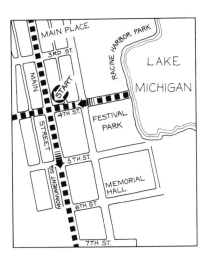

Best Season: Spring, summer, fall.

Length: Varies, but plan on spending at least half a day exploring Racine and the waterfront.

Degree of Difficulty: Easy.

Highlights: Waterfront views and charming shops in the historic district combine to make this a scenic and interesting walk.

Lake Michigan, at 307 miles long and 118 miles wide, is the third largest of the Great Lakes. This walk along the Racine Harbor provides a wonderful view of the lake as well as a chance to visit downtown Racine, a fascinating historic district that nominator Joan Volmut says, "brings back memories of days gone past and at the same time shows signs of progress towards the future."

From the Visitors' Center, walk down Main Street to Monument Square between Fifth and Sixth streets. Originally called Haymarket Square, this was the area where farmers used to gather to sell their produce. Many of the buildings here date back to the mid-1800s. Take your time exploring the many picturesque shops, art galleries, and restaurants before walking along the Fourth Street Causeway to Festival Park, a five-acre city park which boasts a 60 × 120 foot refrigerated ice skating rink.

From Festival Park, continue out along the Causeway to Racine Harbor Park and Reefpoint Marina, a 110-acre recreation area that is the largest on Lake Michigan. In addition to 1,000 boat slips, you'll find a lakefront restaurant here and an observation point for viewing the numerous activities on the water. For an interesting change of pace, you may want to dine aboard the newest luxury yacht, the *Celebration*, docked at Reefpoint Marina.

Before you leave Racine, be sure to sample the *Kringle*, sometimes called "Racine's Global Ambassador" because of its worldwide popularity. This deliciously delicate Danish pastry filled with a variety of fruits or nuts comes from original family recipes handed down over generations by the large Danish population that settled in Racine. The Kringle is responsible for Racine's designation as the "Danish Pastry Capital of the United States."

SOUTH CENTRAL WISCONSIN

Beloit Mall (96)

Directions: Go to the corner of Henry Avenue and Highway 51 north in Beloit.

Best Season: Year-round; mall is indoors and climate-controlled.

Length: One time around the mall takes about seven minutes.

Degree of Difficulty: Easy.

Highlights: According to nominator Roger Schwebke, this is quite simply "the best place in town to walk."

Mall walking is quickly becoming a popular American pastime, but perhaps nowhere is it as much fun as it is in Beloit. Here the doors open to walkers at 8 a.m. Monday through Friday and at 11 a.m. on Sundays and holidays. In marked contrast to some indoor malls where the "walker" takes a distant second place to the "shopper," in the Beloit Mall walkers are warmly welcomed and encouraged. There are many places to rest, if necessary, and the Beloit Memorial Hospital has posted warm-up and exercise signs along the route. Woolworth's and Walgreen's have become gathering places for coffee and talk after walking, and Walgreen's even offers a walker's discount on coffee.

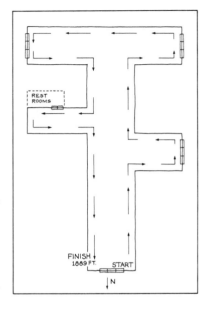

Roger Schwebke, who nominated this walk, has been doing it for six years. "On an average winter day," he says, "there are about seventy walkers, some fast, some slow, some young, some old. Everybody talks to one another, and most of us know each other by name. If you don't show up for several days, somebody will check to see if you've had a problem. Recently while in the hospital, I had visits and cards from many of the walkers. They're a great bunch of people."

It sure sounds like it. Visit the mall and see for yourself, and be sure to ask around for Roger.

SOUTH CENTRAL WISCONSIN

Lake Geneva (97)

Directions: The shore of Lake Geneva is located on Highways 50 and 120. You can pick up the path at numerous points, including: Big Foot Beach Park; Lake Geneva's Library Park; Williams Bay Beach;

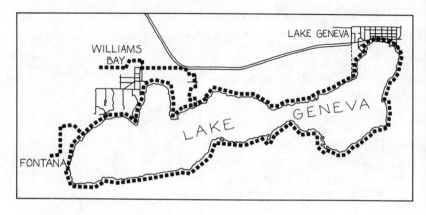

Fontana Beach; Chapin Road, between Conference Point and the Narrows on the North Shore; and Linn Pier Road.

Best Season: Spring, summer, and fall.

Length: 26 miles around the lake.

Degree of Difficulty: Moderate; the path along the shoreline is fairly level. If you go the distance and walk all around the lake, good walking shoes are recommended.

Highlights: A nostalgic walk along the shore of Lake Geneva with lovely views of stately mansions and elegant yachts.

According to legend, Lake Geneva's original name, Big Foot, was chosen because of the lake's unique shape. Long before the first Europeans explored the shores of Lake Superior, the Potawatomi Indians lived around Lake Geneva. Jayne Hoffmann, who nominated this walk, tells us that the trail around the lake still follows the path originally established by the Potawatomi.

Nevertheless, it's not hard to imagine the look of surprise that would appear on a Potawatomi's face if he could see the millionaire mansions now standing on the grounds of his tiny village. And, if our imaginary Potawatomi should happen to glance over the waters, he could not help but gasp at the sight of an antique cruise boat or splendid yacht. He might even catch a wide-eyed glimpse of the *Ada'E*, an impressive old yacht belonging to the Wrigleys. But, of course, knowing nothing of chewing gum or baseball or modern civilization, our Indian friend might conclude that it is much wiser and safer not to tempt the sea serpent.

The relationship between hikers and mansion owners has not always been harmonious, and there have been attempts in the past on the part of home owners to discourage people from walking on the lake path. In a recent court decision, however, it was ruled that since the path was there before the wealthy owners of relatively new mansions, the public had a right to use it "for foot and bicycle travel." This "right of passage" on the lake trail has been respected by all concerned and remains the best way to catch a glimpse of the lifestyle of a bygone era. The lakefront estates were built primarily by the tycoons of the midwest shortly after the Chicago Fire of 1871. Their physical presence, architectural diversity, and well-manicured grounds provide a splendid panorama as you walk along the shores of this peaceful lake.

Jayne Hoffmann enthusiastically recommends the Lake Geneva walk. "It is one of the most interesting walks I have ever taken," she says. "Not only is there beautiful natural scenery to behold, but also magnificent mansions and boats and yachts to watch. The towns along the route make it very convenient for food and rest stops. I cannot encourage you enough to take this wonderful historic walk."

SOUTH CENTRAL WISCONSIN

Picnic Point on Lake Mendota, Madison (98)

Directions: Take I-94 to Highways 12 and 18. Exit at Park Street and follow to the end to the University of Wisconsin's Student Union. Parking is available in the vicinity.

Best Season: Year-round; there is cross-country skiing in winter. Nominator Ronda Allen suggests you bring mosquito repellent during the peak summer weeks.

Length: 6½ miles round-trip from the Student Union out to the point and back. The point itself is 2 miles round-trip.

Degree of Difficulty: Easy; flat paths follow Lake Mendota's shores.

Highlights: A scenic lakeside walk in the midst of a shoreline college campus, said to be one of the most beautiful in the midwest.

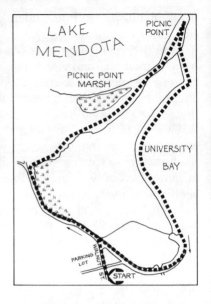

The Picnic Point Trail snakes its way through the middle of a tiny peninsula that juts out into Lake Mendota and is so narrow that at times the lake can be seen on both sides. "It's God's country," says Ronda Allen, who sent us the walk.

Begin at the University of Wisconsin Student Union and follow the trail through a wooded area, past docks and dormitories and beautiful marshland, to a gate which marks the beginning of Picnic Point. You'll get wonderful views of the lake, Ronda tells us, and there's always something going on. It's a great place for bird watching, for example, and the University of Wisconsin Athletic Club called The Hoofers sails and windsurfs on the lake.

After your walk on Picnic Point, Ronda suggests you visit the University of Wisconsin–Madison Arboretum which has 20 miles of trails and fire lanes. The arboretum, which began in 1932 with the purchase of a 245-acre farm, now covers 1,260 acres. Aldo Leopold, the arboretum's first research director, envisioned that it would eventually become, "a sample of what Dane County looked like when our ancestors arrived here." It was an ambitious goal, for by the turn of the century, most of Wisconsin's native plant communities had disappeared. Prairie restoration has been the most successful. More than 300 species of prairie plants bloom in succession from March to November. There are also conifer and hardwood forest restorations, as well as wetlands.

Some areas in the arboretum were not disturbed by the encroachment of humankind, and they have been left alone. One such area is Noe Woods, an oak forest which serves as a benchmark for researchers to assess the condition of other oak forests and to study their long-term development. Numerous questions must still be answered. For example, What will happen when the dominant oaks succumb to disease and wind damage? Will young oaks replace them? Or will Noe Woods disappear after one generation of trees? Students from the University of Wisconsin have been tracking the oaks in Noe Woods since 1951, keeping valuable records that will provide needed insight into oak forest development across the country.

For the walker, Noe Woods can be enjoyed for the peaceful beauty it affords; the wonderful smells of the forest, the leafy canopy rustling overhead, and the wildlife—such as deer, squirrels, rabbits and mice as well as the many species of wildflowers.

There is also a spectacular horticultural area in the arboretum called Longenecker Gardens where you can walk through formal displays of flowering trees and plants as well as forests of pine, fir, spruce, and juniper.

For information about the walking trails in the arboretum, write: The McKay Center, The University of Wisconsin–Madison Arboretum, 1207 Seminole Highway, Madison, Wisconsin 53711, or call (608) 263-7888.

NORTHWESTERN WISCONSIN

Amnicon Falls Walk (99)

Directions: The walk is located in Amnicon Falls State Park, southeast of Superior, Wisconsin, on Highway 2.

Best Season: The park is open from April through September. Nominator John Semo likes to walk here in May when the river is highest and the falls are at their most spectacular. Stop at the office before you begin your walk to pick up the required permit.

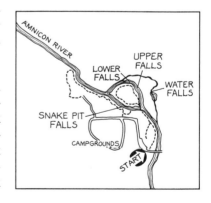

Length: There are several hiking trails throughout the park, ranging from ½ to ¾ mile.

Degree of Difficulty: Easy.

Highlights: This is a wonderful walk through forests and over a covered bridge. But the best part is the cascading beauty of the falls.

Within Amnicon Falls State Park there is a steplike fault in the 600-million-year-old sandstone that forms the foundation for most of this area of Wisconsin. This break, which runs from near Minneapolis, Minnesota, to Ashland, Wisconsin, is mostly underground. But in Douglas County, Wisconsin, part of it is exposed, and perhaps nowhere is it more dramatically exposed than at Amnicon Falls. Here the Amnicon River, which empties into Lake Superior just a few miles away, rushes over huge boulders in a spectacular cascade of white foam.

John Semo particularly likes a particular half-mile trail that parallels the river and passes through a forest of white pine, aspen, maple, and spruce, crosses over the river on one of the few covered bridges in Wisconsin, and leads to a small island where John says, "You have delightful views of the tumbling waters."

In addition to the spectacular waterfalls, Amnicon Falls State Park is home to a wide variety of wildlife. You may see deer, coyote, fox, raccoon, porcupine, and a number of smaller animals on your walk through the park. Along the river look for beaver, mink, and otter. And don't forget the birds. The best time to see and hear them is early in the morning.

The Amnicon River (the name comes from Indian words which mean "where fish spawn") is one of the major streams on the south shore of Lake Superior, and it is still an important spawning river for fish from Lake Superior, the world's largest freshwater lake. In the heart of the park, the river separates into two streams and plunges over three waterfalls of nearly thirty feet each. Sometimes, when there is a particularly good water flow, the river produces a fourth waterfall.

The river is a popular fishing area, so if you like to fish, check in with the park office for current information on seasons, size and bag limits. Everyone 16 years old and older must have a fishing license. Also, if you fish for trout, you must have a Wisconsin trout stamp. If you are really an avid lover of fishing, you may want to drive east on Route 2 to the town of Brule where trout swim in the Brule River. The river has enticed a number of "fishing" presidents, including Ulysses S. Grant, Calvin Coolidge, and Dwight D. Eisenhower and has thus earned the nickname "River of Presidents."

EAST CENTRAL WISCONSIN

Hussong Trail, Green Bay (100)

Directions: The trail is located in the Bay Beach Wildlife Sanctuary, 2 miles from downtown Green Bay. Exit I-43 at Webster Avenue, and stop at the main Nature Center for information as to which birds are in town and what's in bloom.

Best Season: May and June, when the waterfowl are hatching and the wildflowers are in bloom.

Length: One mile, but you can easily spend half a day exploring this wonderful place.

Degree of Difficulty: Easy.

Highlights: A variety of landscapes with plenty of information to enhance your appreciation make this trail a perfect place for a family outing.

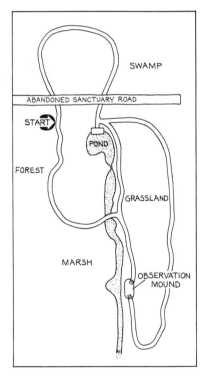

The Hussong Trail, which derives its name from a local biologist and conservationist, is nominator Ty Baumann's favorite walk in the sanctuary because of its interesting variety. It begins in a forested area where you might happen upon a red fox, some white-tailed deer, weasel, mink, chipmunk ("the kids' favorite," Ty says), groundhog, and raccoon. From the forest, the trail enters a cattail marsh where walkers have access to the wetlands via a boardwalk. "This really adds to the experience," Ty says, "allowing everyone to see the marsh up close, instead of just from a distant bank."

At the end of the marsh is one of the many lagoons scattered throughout the sanctuary (there are 55 acres of water in the park). Here you can see the endangered common and forester terns, as well as a variety of other waterfowl (3,000 visit the sanctuary during the winter), including black-crowned night herons, ducks, and Canada geese. Ty and his wife go on bird hikes every Thursday and Saturday morning from mid-April through May and invite you to come along. You'll see some interesting reptiles as well: rare turtles and garter, hognose, and brown snakes.

A hard-surface trail called Web of Life Trail runs from the Nature Center to an observation building where you can watch the waterfowl and feed the ducks from a "duck shack." Several stations along the short trail discuss the wetlands and their relationship to people. A large web illustrates the "Web of Life." The trail, with its emphasis on education, is geared toward children. "This is a family-oriented sanctuary," Ty explains, "a great place to give kids an appreciation of nature."

BEST WALK NOMINATION FORM
(Please use additional paper when necessary)

Type and name of walk: _____

Region: _____

How to get there from the highway: _____

_____

Why selected: _____

Degree of difficulty: (Easy, moderate, moderately difficult, difficult, very difficult) Why? _____

Best time of year to go:_____

Description of walk (please include map and black-and-white photo if possible) _____

Physical environment: _____

Points of interest along the route (including interesting people you might meet along the way). Please include a statement of fifty words or more and/or a brochure: _____

_____

Walking time and distance: _____

Any warnings or hazards? _____

Personal statement: Your experiences during the walk (please include a statement of fifty words or more): _____

_____

Additional comments or information: _____

_____

The information I have provided is true to the best of my knowledge. I understand and agree that this information and materials become the property of Walking World, to be used at its discretion. I also agree that my name can be used in connection with the publication of the walk.

_____
(Signature)

(Please print):   Name: _____

Address: _____

Telephone: _____

Please send to: *Walking World*
P.O. Box K, Gracie Station
New York, NY 10028

ABOUT THE AUTHORS

Gary Yanker has been dubbed walking's foremost authority in America, Europe, and Japan by *USA Today*, *The New York Times*, NBC News, Japan's *Asahi Shinhum* and Germany's *Frankfurter Allgemeine*, among others. His six previous bestselling walking books and tapes, including *The Complete Book of Exercisewalking* and *Walking Workouts*, have sold over 500 million copies worldwide. He has served as the walking editor for both *American Health* and *Prevention* magazines and helped found Walking World.

Carol D. Tarlow is a former senior editor of Reader's Digest Condensed Books. She is co-author, with Gary Yanker, of *America's Greatest Walks*. She heads her own writing and editing business in California.